Reading Basics for All Teachers

Reading Basics for All Teachers

Supporting All Learners

Second Edition

Lin Carver and Lauren Pantoja

ROWMAN & LITTLEFIELD
Lanham • Boulder • New York • London

Published by Rowman & Littlefield
A wholly owned subsidiary of The Rowman & Littlefield Publishing Group, Inc.
4501 Forbes Boulevard, Suite 200, Lanham, Maryland 20706
www.rowman.com

6 Tinworth Street, London SE11 5AL, United Kingdom

British Library Cataloguing in Publication Information Available

Library of Congress Cataloging-in-Publication Data
Names: Carver, Lin, 1955- author. | Pantoja, Lauren, 1953- author.
Title: Reading basics for all teachers : supporting all learners / Lin Carver and Lauren Pantoja.
Description: Second edition. | Lanham : Rowman & Littlefield, [2020] | Includes bibliographical references and index. | Summary: "This books helps teachers understand how to motivate and engage students so that they think critically about text"—Provided by publisher.
Identifiers: LCCN 2019059531 (print) | LCCN 2019059532 (ebook) | ISBN 9781475854695 (cloth) | ISBN 9781475854701 (paperback) | ISBN 9781475854718 (epub)
Subjects: LCSH: Reading (Elementary)—United States. | Language arts (Elementary)—United States.
Classification: LCC LB1573 .C326 2020 (print) | LCC LB1573 (ebook) | DDC 372.4—dc23
LC record available at https://lccn.loc.gov/2019059531
LC ebook record available at https://lccn.loc.gov/2019059532

This book is dedicated to all the teachers, coaches, and administrators who make a difference in the lives of students every day.

Contents

Preface

Literacy is the basic building block for all instruction. Without proficient reading and critical thinking skills, students are limited in their ability to access information. Teaching reading is a complex process that requires teachers to have a thorough understanding of oral language, phonological awareness, phonics, vocabulary, fluency, and comprehension and instructional strategies for teaching these components. Additionally, teachers need to understand how to motivate and engage students so that they think critically about text. New to this edition are updated strategies and research including expanded information for secondary learners, ELLs, and writing instruction to support reading comprehension.

Acknowledgments

Our most sincere thanks to Carlie Wall and the editors of this book for going above and beyond to help make this book a success.

Chapter 1

The Literacy Mosaic

LITERARY CONNECTION

The grandpa held the jar of honey so that all the family could see, then
  dipped a ladle into it and drizzled honey on the cover of a small book.
Then he handed the book to her. "Taste!"
She dipped her finger into the honey and put it into her mouth.
"What is that taste?" the grandma asked.
The little girl answered, "Sweet!"
Then all of the family said in a single voice, "Yes, and so is
  knowledge, but knowledge is like the bee that made that sweet
  honey, you have to chase it through the pages of a book!"
The little girl knew that the promise to read was at last hers. (Polacco, 2001, p. 1)

All of our students enter school with the expectation, the promise, of learning to read. As students enter kindergarten, the varied developmental stages of individuals are evident from day one. Some enter school with a strong background in the alphabetic principle, phonological awareness, phonics, and vocabulary from lots of word play and experiences with print at an early age. Many even enter kindergarten prepared to learn to read and write. Others enter school with learning challenges or limited experiences with sounds, words, and print. Fine motor abilities, social skills, and the ability to concentrate for longer periods of time can also vary.

Kindergarten and first-grade teachers have expressed concerns that students entering school do not all begin at the same "starting line." These differences can impact the progress and motivation of students as they move through school and cause gaps in literacy development.

Patricia Polacco (2001) described her own experience with learning to read in the poignant picture book *Thank You, Mr. Falker.* She described her reading experience as she progressed through the grades as "just plain torture." She "hated, hated, hated school." It was her fifth-grade teachers, Mr. Falker and Miss Plessy, a reading teacher, who changed her life and helped her succeed as a reader. In today's world, many different kinds of readers can be found in our elementary and secondary classrooms.

CLASSROOM VISIT

Mrs. Smith gazed around her third-grade class. The first three weeks of school had been eye-opening to say the least. Her vision of twenty-five students opening their textbooks and becoming absorbed in the assigned reading had quickly disintegrated!

"Class, open your books to page 11, read Chapter 2 and then answer the questions at the end of the chapter. Christine, Rashad, Thomas, and Rosa, could you bring your books back to the reading table?" The four students straggled to the back table halfheartedly. They slouched into their chairs and dropped their books onto the table. Mrs. Smith smiled encouragingly at them and said, "Please open your books to page 11, and let's read this section together. Christine, could you read the first sentence for us?"

Christine began slowly, struggling to produce the phonemes in each word, "M..a..r..c..o P..o..l..o..s left Ven..ice and re..m..a..i..n..ed in Ch..i..n..a for 17 long y..e..a..r..s."

Mrs. Smith listened patiently, quieting the other students as they began to fidget in their seats. When Christine finished the last word, she proudly looked up at Mrs. Smith, who smiled reassuringly and addressed the group. "Everyone put your finger on the name in the next sentence. Does anyone think they can pronounce it?" Everyone stared quietly at the page. "The name is Kublai Khan. Please repeat it."

"Kublai Khan," they all responded somewhat in unison.

"Good. Rashad, will you continue?" Mrs. Smith asked.

"They often wanted to return home, Kublai Khan did not give them per.. mitted," he responded without realizing that he had read anything incorrectly.

Christine's hand waved in the air. "Can I read?" she pleaded.

Mrs. Smith smiled and said to Christine, "It's Rashad's turn, Christine, let him continue."

"When . . . he finally . . . returned. He . . . was imprisoned and told . . . his . . . stories to . . . a cellmate." He read grouping the words sporadically while rushing through the punctuation.

"Thomas, please continue," Mrs. Smith requested.

"He had to be parents," Thomas read, oblivious to the fact that "parents" made no sense in the context of the passage.

"Rosa, your turn," Mrs. Smith directed.

"He tried to be patient, but it was hard. He missed his family, but he finally was released," Rosa read fluently and with expression.

"OK, everyone, look back in the passage and put your finger under the word that tells you where the passage takes place," Mrs. Smith directed, trying to ascertain what they understood from the reading. "Great job, Thomas and Rosa," observed Mrs. Smith to the two students who confidently found the answer. "Rosa, why did Marco Polo have trouble being patient?" asked Mrs. Smith.

"I don't know. It doesn't say," mumbled Rosa.

And so the lesson went. This was a grade-level text; surely, they can't really need this much help with it, Mrs. Smith thought. But they did. Mrs. Smith wondered how she would meet the differing needs of each of her students.

LITERACY DEVELOPMENT

Many children learn to read without any difficulty; however, others struggle for many years trying to master this process. In fact, according to the data from the National Assessment of Educational Progress, 33 percent of the fourth graders in the United States scored below the basic level during the 2011 reading assessment period (NCES, 2012). Consequently, approximately one-third of the students in the typical classroom have only partial proficiency with grade-level, fundamental reading skills.

These reading difficulties are evidenced in a variety of ways. Some students substitute words or phrases while they are reading. Others stumble clumsily through a text, lacking fluency. Some appear to read fluently but can't seem to remember the content of what they read. At other times, struggling readers appear to be just reading word by word rather than actually processing the information from the text. They struggle with automaticity, which means they have difficulty with automatic word recognition. This impacts fluency and ultimately comprehension of the text. As teachers, we need to help each of these struggling readers close the gaps in their literacy development and become proficient readers. Emphasis on grade-level complex text continues to increase (Hiebert, 2011a), and there has been increasing evidence that if we want our struggling readers to make progress toward proficiency, they need exposure to and practice with grade-level complex text. "Supporters of increasing text complexity have argued that easier, ability-matched text "ultimately denies students the very language, information, and modes of thought they need most to move up and on" (Reynolds & Goodwin, 2016, p. 1). Hiebert and Mesmer (2013) indicated that the importance of increased text complexity is more significant at the middle and high school levels because in the past fifty years it is at these levels where text complexity has decreased. It is important to remember, however, that younger readers may be vulnerable if texts become more challenging without teachers providing the necessary support. There is a fine line between productive struggle and frustration. Sanden (2014) explains that subjecting students to constant struggle with texts at their frustration level may affect their motivation to read (Reynolds & Goodwin, 2016). Properly supporting students as they read complex texts can move a frustrating experience into a successful one. Students who experience reading difficulties in the early grades often are unable to close the resulting achievement gap (Kelly & Campbell, 2010) that widens as they progress through school. Teachers must be able to recognize students' foundational areas of need and provide diagnostic and prescriptive literacy support. What makes the difference between proficient and struggling readers?

The differences between proficient and struggling readers can sometimes be seen as early as first grade. During first grade, proficient readers will have been exposed to approximately 18,681 words of connected text; however, struggling readers will see only approximately 9,975 words (Tankersley, 2005). So even though these struggling readers may be developing reading skills, they are not keeping up with their grade-level peers. As the struggling readers progress through additional years of schooling, the gap between their reading level and the level of their grade-level peers continues to widen.

At other times, students who seem to be progressing normally in their reading skills through the primary grades suddenly appear to begin struggling around fourth grade. This phenomenon is often referred to as the "fourth grade slump." It can be caused by the following factors or by any combination of these factors: an actual deficit in foundational reading skills, the reduction of pictorial clues within the text, an increase in the vocabulary demands, and/or a greater emphasis on textual comprehension in the intermediate grades with a decreased emphasis on foundational reading skills. Others believe the slump is due to difficulties that students are experiencing in processing and comprehending the more complex sentences used in intermediate-grade texts. This increased emphasis on complex comprehension and critical thinking skills can make comprehension more difficult for some children (Sanacore & Palumbo, 2009). Each of these factors could impact a student's reading development.

Literacy Development as a Physiological Process

Literacy development is first and foremost a physiological process. Its development depends on the brain being able to receive visual and auditory signals from the environment. The reader must be able to focus on the printed symbols, track from left to right across the paper, discriminate between slight visual differences, distinguish between figure and ground, and have the visual acuity and ability to process this information. In addition, the learner must be able to distinguish between slight differences in the sounds (phonemes) and units of meaning (morphemes) of the language. For example, he must be able to hear and distinguish differences between phonemes /e/ and /i/, such as in "pen" and "pin," so that he understands the difference between "Hand me the pen" and "Hand me the pin." Poverty and positive or negative home environments could play a crucial role in students' overall health and growth as well. Good health, visual and auditory acuity, and well-developed perceptual skills affect the reading process.

Literacy Development as a Linguistic Process

The foundational skills for literacy are carefully shaped throughout the child's preschool and primary years through various experiences that contribute to literacy development. Literacy is a language process that incorporates oral and written skills through various cueing systems to form the overall literacy mosaic. A mosaic includes many pieces merged together to form a pattern or a unified whole. The literacy process is much the same. The physical, psychological, social, mental, and language processes all combine to form the fluent reader. The cueing systems combine facets of these processes together. The cueing systems describe the way that the information is being processed. Students use five different cueing systems as they process the printed text: the syntactic, semantic, schematic, graphophonic, and pragmatic cueing systems.

For example, a student might encounter the unknown word "cement" in the following sentence: "The boy fell off of his bike onto the *cement.*" The syntactic cueing system informs the student that the unknown word is probably a noun or a thing. This system provides the student with a clue as to the part of speech that would make sense in the sentence, even if the student cannot actually name the part of speech. Based on his proficiency with the English language, the reader understands the word's function in the sentence. If the reader is not proficient with the English language, the syntactic system is not as helpful.

The semantic cueing system helps the student identify possible words that would make sense in the sentence. In our sample sentence, "The boy fell off of his bike onto the *cement,*" a few of these possibilities could include the sidewalk, street, path, or driveway because the student knows from experience that these would all be possible places to ride his bike.

The schematic cueing system builds on the semantic system because it is the use of information based on the reader's prior knowledge or personal experience. For example, there might not be any bike paths or sidewalks where our reader can ride, so based upon his personal experience he would probably not choose those words to complete the sentence.

The graphophonic cueing system helps the reader to be able to match the symbol with the sound it would produce. The student can use this cueing system to decode the word "cement." In this case, a reader who has a well-developed graphophonic system realizes that the letter "c" followed by "e" usually makes an /s/ sound, so he could rule out the choices *path* and *driveway* since they don't begin with an /s/ sound.

The last cueing system is the pragmatic cueing system. This system relates to the use of language in the social, cultural, and regional contexts. In our example, "The boy fell off of his bike onto the *cement,*" his choices would be limited by the words used in his particular setting. "Macadam," another word used to describe a road surface, would probably not be one of the choices our reader considered because it was not a word used within his particular region, even though it is a possible word choice.

Literacy Development as a Cognitive Process

Literacy development is also a cognitive process. Successful literacy development requires that students effectively integrate a variety of personal and literary experiences and skills. Students must have the cognitive ability necessary to combine these into an organized whole to increase their understanding of text.

Recent discoveries in neuroscience have identified important principles of learning. The first principle is that learning depends on the integration of brain hemisphere structures (Lyons, 2003). For the majority of individuals, the left hemisphere of the brain is responsible for speech and writing, although research seems to indicate that the brain might not be as specialized for comprehending language as it is for producing it. Literacy development requires both hemispheres. The right hemisphere is particularly adept at processing whole information such as faces, pictures, and three-dimensional objects. Verbal memories about words and experiences are stored in the left hemisphere, whereas visual memories of words are stored in the right.

The second principle is that neural development is continuous. One of the ways that the brain grows is through myelination of axons. Myelin, a white fatty insulating substance, insulates the neurons and helps to facilitate the processing of information between the right and the left hemispheres of the brain. Repetitions of a process, such as reading, increase the amount of myelin. The more myelin that is built up, the more automatic the process becomes. Learning requires that many groups of neurons located in specific parts of the brain need to work in unison to produce single actions such as reading. When a child is born, there is very little myelin. In fact, it is estimated to take twenty to thirty years to finish this myelination process (Lyons, 2003). Consequently, early childhood experiences, conversations, and repeated practice play important roles in learning to read. Even more important for our struggling readers is the finding that suggests that "human beings have an unlimited potential for learning that continues through old age" (Lyons, 2003, p. 13). Struggling readers, no matter what their age, need additional practice to build the myelin that will increase automaticity in reading.

Literacy Development as a Psychological Process

In addition, literacy is a psychological or motivational process. Students must want to mature and grow in literacy. Students must have the desire to learn and be willing to take the risks necessary for learning. One important aspect of the psychological process is creating an environment that is emotionally and physically safe. Motivation is a key area to consider for struggling readers because teachers often express that motivation is one of the greatest challenges they face with their striving learners. Finding a way to help students be successful will increase their willingness to take risks.

Literacy Development as a Social and Cultural Process

Finally, literacy is a social and cultural process. Literacy development begins through social interactions between the child and her caregiver and significant others. Read alouds, which can provide the foundations for the reading process, are a social activity that allows for interactions between both parties. Forming meaning occurs as a result of discussions related to the text. Vygotsky's social developmental theory (1978) states that social interaction provides the foundation for cognitive development and learning ("Learning Theories," 2013).

In addition, readers' culture and personal experiences contribute to their understanding of the text. In a study by Steffenson et al. (1979), nineteen students from India and twenty students from the United States read two different passages about weddings. One passage described a wedding in India, and another described an American wedding. Students from India remembered more information from the passage about the Indian wedding ceremony than they did about the American wedding ceremony. The opposite was true of the students from the United States. This study illustrated that culture affects the amount and type of information that is processed and remembered.

STAGES OF READING DEVELOPMENT

As students combine and refine the various skills they are developing in the physiological, linguistic, cognitive, psychological, cultural, and social areas, these impact their progress through the stages of reading development.

Literacy skills develop along a continuum based upon students' experiences rather than their chronological age or grade level. An understanding of the stages is helpful in determining student expectations, choosing appropriate texts, and identifying instructional strategies. These stages have different names, depending on what resource you are reading. In addition, there is also variation in abilities between students within the same stage. We have identified four broad stages along the reading continuum on the elementary level and two stages on the secondary level. However, these stages could be divided into additional smaller categories or stages (Pacific Resources for Education and Learning, 2012). For each stage, we will identify the student characteristics, the focus or goals, and the text features. These stages align closely to Chall's (1983) six stages of reading.

Emergent Reader

Emergent readers are generally found in prekindergarten to kindergarten classrooms. These students typically have very limited phonemic awareness and know less than half of the alphabet letters. They might recognize a few sight words, but they have not really mastered the concept of words. They are developing an understanding of the concepts of print and enjoy repeated readings of their favorite texts.

The major focus or goal of this stage is to develop the understanding that print conveys a message and that pictures help to support this message. Left-to-right and top-to-bottom directionalities are being introduced along with the concept of a return sweep to the beginning of the next line. The student is learning to match voice to print, determining the difference between letters and words, distinguishing similarities and differences between beginning and ending sounds, and expanding his sight vocabulary to at least ten words.

Text used with readers in this stage should have large, easy-to-see print that is placed consistently on the page with pictures that help to convey the meaning. Text that is predictable with repeated words or phrases will help to engage the emergent reader in the reading process. Single lines of text with one to six words per page will help the reader begin to match words to print. Repeated readings and extending stories by encouraging both print and pictorial responses will help the student to make predictions about the text while improving comprehension.

Beginning Reader

Beginning readers are typically found in the late kindergarten to first-grade classrooms. These readers can generally match sounds to print and understand the concept of words. They can recognize and produce most of the letters of the alphabet and about fifty basic sight words. They can read texts with simple sentence structure but may need pictorial support for understanding. They are developing decoding skills and are typically confident with decoding beginning and ending consonants.

The major goals for this stage are to have the student develop a more extensive sight vocabulary of about 100 words and oral reading fluency of about 10–30 words per minute using appropriate expression, intonation, and phrasing. Learners should also be developing comprehension strategies for predicting, retelling, sequencing, self-monitoring, rereading, and self-correction. During this stage, the readers' use of cueing systems and language patterns is developing, and they are reading for meaning. The reading habit of risk taking while predicting and confirming words based upon meaning is being established.

The texts at this stage tend to be longer, and context clues may be needed to understand the vocabulary. Technical vocabulary is incorporated in addition to compound and two-syllable words. During this stage, texts with medium to small print size using a variety of fonts are appropriate. Sentences are becoming more complex and contain a wider range of verb tenses.

Transitional Reader

Transitional readers are typically found in the second- to third-grade classroom. These readers rely on the teacher for support, but they are working toward becoming independent readers. They have a sight vocabulary of more than 100 words, and they are able to use decoding and comprehension strategies. They can confidently decode one-syllable, short- and long-vowel words containing consonant blends and digraphs. Their reading rate is increasing, and they typically enjoy longer and more complex texts.

The major goals for this stage are expanding word study to include diphthongs and R control vowel sounds; increasing fluency to sixty words per minute with appropriate phrasing, tone, and expression; and continuing the development of comprehension strategies. At this stage, the students generally have developed strategies for figuring out many words, but they continue to need help with understanding the increasingly more difficult text to which they are exposed.

The text used at this stage conveys the major portion of the passage's meaning. Fewer pictures are included, and they generally offer little support. Dialogue, description, and literary language are incorporated into the text. Stories are longer and may involve episodes, short chapters, or series. Texts include multisyllabic and technical vocabulary. An understanding of characters and points of view are beginning to be developed.

Fluent Reader

The fluent reader is generally found beginning at the end of third grade. These readers have the ability to apply various decoding and comprehension strategies. While reading, they monitor and self-correct and can use multiple cueing systems to determine unknown words. They use word parts and context clues to determine meaning. They can read at about 100 words per minute while performing word recognition and comprehension tasks. At this stage, they can skim to retrieve information, and they read and write independently. As well as being able to describe supporting details from narrative and expository texts, they are able to retell main ideas and events.

The major goals of this stage are to continue to develop independence in using comprehension strategies within, between, and among texts. The reader is learning to process information on multiple levels and to form opinions about the information presented in the text. While developing "before, during, and after reading" strategies, they are learning to use textual information to make inferences and draw conclusions.

During this stage, font size in text is typically small with little pictorial support. Plots are becoming more sophisticated, and stories contain abstract or symbolic themes. Characters are more highly developed, and there is an increase in the amount of informational or nonfiction texts used for enjoyment and learning. Texts should include novels, textbooks, reference materials, magazines, newspapers, poetry, classics, and Internet resources.

Reading development is a continuum. A teacher who understands the stages of reading is better able to facilitate this development and has appropriate expectations. Many students progress fluidly through these stages but some do not.

Multiple Perspective

Readers during the Multiple Perspective stage are developing the ability to understand multiple viewpoints. They understand their own perspective and are able to understand that other people or characters might view the same issue differently depending upon their background, experiences, and/or needs. Readers typically develop and refine this ability during their secondary school experiences between the seventh through twelfth grades. During this stage students are exposed to a broader range of complex materials which contain a variety of viewpoints. Readers are expanding their vocabulary through the systematic study of words and word parts.

Worldview

During college and beyond, readers are expanding their reading to meet their own needs and for their own purposes. Through this process they are integrating and synthesizing their own knowledge with those ideas presented by others to create new information and to refine ideas.

CREATING THE LITERACY MOSAIC

Proficient readers differ from struggling readers in that they have well-developed phonological and phonics skills, read fluently, have extensive vocabulary, understand the meaning of grade-level texts, and can analyze information between and among texts. Difficulties in even one of these basic areas can significantly impact successful reading development. These foundational pieces are combined to produce the mosaic of a proficient grade-level reader.

All of these foundational pieces need to be addressed in order for students to be prepared for the reading demands they will face during their school experience and beyond. Simply increasing the complexity of texts used within the classroom will not increase your struggling readers' text capacity. As teachers, we need to provide opportunities for these learners to build foundational skills. For students to be able to comprehend a text, they need to be able to understand more than 90 percent of the words within that text (Hiebert, 2011a). This is why addressing these foundational skills is so essential.

These foundational skills provide the basis for the reading process, and they are necessary for students to be able to handle the "increasingly more rigorous text and vocabulary" to which they are exposed with the implementation of more rigorous standards (Oregon Literacy Plan, n.d., p. F-3). Foundational skills, however, are not developed in isolation. "Instruction in foundation skills should occur in concert with instruction related to reading, writing, speaking and listening, and language" (IRA, n.d., p. 2). While students are developing strong vocabulary and comprehension skills by reading and listening to narrative and informational text, they also need to be developing strong foundational skills that include print concepts, phonological awareness, phonics, word recognition, and fluency. However, due to physical, maturational, social, academic, cognitive, or emotional issues, this necessary development may not have occurred with our striving readers because they might not have been ready to process the information when it was presented.

PLANNING FOR INSTRUCTION

Now you have these struggling readers in your room who may lack the skills they need to read confidently. You, as their teacher, want to make a difference by helping them close the gaps so that they can be successful. But what can you do? The years of unsuccessful reading have widened the academic gap between where they are and where they need to be. Additionally, with struggling readers, these academic gaps may contribute to motivational issues. These students have been unsuccessful enough times that they do not like reading, or they may think that it is boring, or they just can't do it. Consequently, they give up and lack the motivation to engage in the reading process (Beers, 2003).

With the increased emphasis on data-based student performance and increasingly rigorous standards, instructional shifts are occurring and students are being held to more stringent expectations. Building student knowledge using content area texts has become a central feature of instruction. Students are expected to be able to build content knowledge by grappling with difficult text rather than through teacher presentation of the information. Teachers are creating text sets to build background knowledge, support complex topics, and balance the use of informational and literary texts.

For our struggling readers, this can be a help and a hindrance. We need to find ways to scaffold them through these texts so that they are able to build their content knowledge (NYC Gov, n.d.), increase their knowledge of and handle more extensive vocabulary, and use evidence from the text in the reading and writing processes. This increased volume of reading on a topic will theoretically build that content knowledge and vocabulary in support of comprehension, but our struggling readers who often lack the motivation to read because it is difficult for them, need social and emotional support so they can persevere. The emphasis on complex text has increased the demands and expectations for our struggling readers and has changed instructional practices through the use of text-based questions and writing that emphasize using textual information to support student answers (NYSED, 2013). If students struggle with reading the text, they will have difficulty with these tasks. We must be strategic in selecting and scaffolding students through the volume of reading that is necessary in the development of literate, college- and career-ready students.

We must also take into consideration our diverse school populations. Many of our schools have large numbers of English language learners (ELLs) who are held to the same standards as their English-speaking counterparts. The study mentioned earlier in this chapter about the students from India and the United States who read two different passages about weddings from their respective countries found that students remembered more information from the passages about which they had more background knowledge. This supports the importance of building knowledge and vocabulary for our ELLs to help them succeed as readers of English. When selecting texts to build background knowledge and vocabulary, we must take into consideration the cultural differences of our ELLs to provide them equitable opportunities for comprehending the selected texts. Our ELLs use their first language experiences to make sense of texts in the second language. Therefore, they will need even greater social and emotional supports and opportunities to connect their prior experiences to reading because their experiences and vocabulary knowledge differ from those of their English-speaking peers (Holmes, Rutledge, & Gauthier, 2009).

WHAT MAKES TEXT COMPLEX?

One factor that might make text complex is the readability. Many different formulas have been used to measure this variable. However, each method uses quantitative features within the text, such as the number of syllables per word and the sentence or word lengths, to calculate the readability. Lexile is one measure that has been used to help match readers with text. However, just because books have the same Lexile measures does not mean that they have the same ease of reading. *Harry Potter and the Chamber of Secrets* and *The Old Man and the Sea* both have a Lexile of 940. The style and content of *Harry Potter* are easier for students to understand than the content of *The Old Man and the Sea*, even though both books have the same Lexile level (Hiebert, 2011b). Quantitative features alone are not enough to determine the complexity of the text.

Text complexity is more than readability. A text may have a lower readability score and still be very complex. The factors of text complexity have been visualized as a triangle. Quantitative factors represent one side of the Common Core complexity triangle. The Common Core State Standards Initiative has identified the other factors that should also be considered when determining the complexity of the text. The second side of the triangle is composed of qualitative factors. These features are more difficult to measure. They would include text structures such as subplots and time shifts, language features such as figurative or archaic language and sentence structure, levels of meaning, and knowledge demands. The final side is composed of reader and task features. These would include such factors as the reader's cognitive capabilities, motivation, purpose for reading, and previous experiences.

Today's standards place an emphasis on vocabulary and comprehension skills for intermediate students. However, all individuals do not learn in the same way or at the same time. Struggling readers may still need support in the foundational skills of phonics, phonemic awareness, and fluency while they are learning to master the comprehension and vocabulary standards. This is why it is important to consider the foundational standards for struggling older readers as well as our elementary students.

All readers, whether struggling or proficient, are developing and refining their reading skills as they encounter various genres and complexities in texts. Students may be more fluent when reading one type of text rather than another. A student who easily comprehends literature may not be as skilled at comprehending a science text, while another student may thrive on informational text but experience difficulty when engaging with narrative texts. Our receptive and expressive vocabularies are continuously expanding, and comprehension strategies are continuously being refined. Reading is a lifelong skill that needs to be continuously nurtured. What was learned about reading in elementary school is not enough to create successful twenty-first-century adults who are college and career ready. Teachers throughout the K–12 system need to be the impetus that prepares our students for their future in both college and careers, and they need to provide a continuous focus on the development of literacy skills in all contents areas. Teachers at all levels make the difference in our students' literacy development!

REFERENCES

Beers, K. (2003). *When Kids Can't Read What Teachers Can Do: A Guide for Teachers 6–12*. Portsmouth, NH: Heinemann.

Chall, J. S. (1983). *Stages of Reading Development*. New York: McGraw-Hill Book Company.

Hiebert, E. H. (2011a). From the vantage point of struggling readers. In *Implementing the Common Core State Standards: Getting to the Core* (session). Orlando, FL: International Reading Association.

Hiebert, E. H. (2011b). Looking "within" the Lexile for more guidance: Word frequency and sentence length. Santa Cruz, CA: Text Project. Retrieved from http://textproject.org/frankly-freddy/looking-within-the-lexile-for-more-guidance-word-frequency-and-sentence-length/.

Hiebert, E., & Mesmer, H. (2013). Upping the ante of text complexity in the common core state standards: Examining its potential impact on young readers. *Educational Researcher, 42*(1), 44–51.

Holmes, K. P., Rutledge, S., & Gauthier, L. R. (2009). Understanding the cultural-linguistic divide in American classrooms: Language learning strategies for a diverse student population. *Reading Horizons, 49*(4). Retrieved from https://scholarworks.wmich.edu/reading_horizons/vol49/iss4/4.

International Reading Association. (n.d.). Literacy implementation guidance for the ELA Common Core State Standards, IRA. Retrieved from http://www.reading.org/Libraries/association-documents/ira_ccss_guidelines.pdf.

Kelly, C., & Campbell, L. (2012). Helping struggling readers. Baltimore: John Hopkins University. Retrieved from http://education.jhu.edu/PD/newhorizons/strategies/topics/literacy/articles/helping-struggling-readers/.

Learning Theories.com. (2013). Social development theory (Vygotsky). Retrieved from http://www.learning-theories.com/vygotskys-social-learning-theory.html.

NCES. (2012). *Digest of Educational Statistics 2012.* Retrieved from http://nces.ed. gov/programs/coe/pdf/coe_cnb.pdf.

NYC Gov. (n.d.). *Crosswalk of Common Core Instructional Shifts: ELA/Literacy.* Retrieved from http://schools.nyc.gov/NR/rdonlyres/058ED42A-2857-4747-8E41- 39BF89BCC374/0/CommonCoreInstructionalShifts_ELALiteracy.pdf.

NYSED. (2013). Common Core shifts. *EngageNY.* Retrieved from http://www.enga geny.org/resource/common-core-shifts.

Oregon State Board of Education. (2009). *Instruction: Oregon K–12 Literacy Framework.* Retrieved from http://www.ode.state.or.us/teachlearn/subjects/elarts/readin g/literacy/chapter-3-instruction.pdf.

Pacific Resources for Education and Learning. (2012). Stages of reading development. *Reading Rockets.* Retrieved from http://www.readingrockets.org/article/st ages-reading-development.

Reynolds, D., & Goodwin, A. (2016). Supporting students reading complex texts: Evidence for motivational scaffolding. *AERA Open.* https://doi.org/10.1177/2 332858416680353.

Sanacore, J., & Palumbo, A. (2009). Understanding the fourth-grade slump: Our point of view. *The Educational Forum, 73,* 67–74. Retrieved from http://www.kdp.org/ publications/theeducationalforum/pdf/sanacore.pdf.

Sanden, S. (2014). Text complexity: A new way forward or two steps back? *English Journal, 25*(2), 7–14.

Steffensen, M. S., Joag-Dev, C., & Anderson, R. C. (1979). A cross-cultural perspective on reading comprehension. *Reading Research Quarterly, 15*(1), 10–15.

Tankersley, K. (2005). *Literacy Strategies for Grades 4–12.* Alexandria, VA: ASCD. Retrieved from http://www.ascd.org/publications/books/104428/chapters/The-S truggling-Reader.aspx.

Chapter 2

Oral Language

CLASSROOM SCENARIO

Mrs. Smith stepped to the next table group with her clipboard in hand to quietly observe the discussion. The students were so involved in their conversation that they didn't even realize she was there. The room was buzzing with student talk about the authenticity of the video *The First Thanksgiving*. They were comparing it to texts they had read about the Wampanoag Native Americans and the first Thanksgiving.

"I thought the Wampanoag were depicted realistically," Thomas said. "They looked like Native Americans." Thomas smiled at the group, looked at Sarah, and said, "Put a mark by the word 'depict' on the vocabulary sheet, Sarah."

"I disagree with your comment that the Wampanoag were depicted realistically, Thomas, because Squanto was wearing almost no clothes. It was winter and it says right here in the third paragraph that the Wampanoag wore deerskin wrapped around them in the winter," Sarah stated. "Now, I get a point for 'depict.'"

Maria looked up at the accountable talk posters on the wall and added, "I would like to add on to what Sarah said about what the Wampanoag wore in the winter. It says in paragraph 3 that they wore leggings in the winter and the men's leggings were long. The man in the video was not wearing anything on his legs."

Sarah nodded as Thomas underlined a sentence in the text. "Sarah," Maria said, "you're supposed to mark on the vocabulary sheet that you used the words Wampanoag and deerskin."

"Keep up the great discussion, guys. What are some other things you noticed about the video that would determine if it is or is not authentic? Thomas, I think the next item on your graphic organizer would be a good point to bring up."

Mrs. Smith moved to the next table feeling very pleased with herself. The practice they had done using the accountable talk posters earlier in the week had really paid off. This discussion was sounding very academic!

LITERARY CONNECTION

As soon as Frankie says it Mom says . . . "You watch ya mout!" Mom says, "Mout," not "mouth." We got a problem here with the "th" sounds. It's not just us—it's all a Brooklyn, maybe Queens, too. My English teacher says I also drop vowels like a bad juggler, and have an infuriating tense problem, whatever that meant. So anyway, if you put the "th" problem and the vowel thing together, our family's Catlick, instead of Catholic, and my name's Antny instead of Anthony. Somehow that got changed into Antsy when I was little, and they've called me Antsy ever since. It don't bother me no more. Used to, but, y'know, you grow into your name. (Shusterman, 2004, p. 3)

ORAL LANGUAGE CONTINUUM

The students in Ms. Smith's class were using academic language in their discussions. Academic language includes the approximately 50,000 words students are expected to have mastered by the end of their high school career (Finley, 2014) and the constructions needed for speaking, grammar, and an understanding of the genres to complete work in academic settings. It includes the vocabulary specific to each content area, as well as the language required for analyzing, synthesizing, and conveying ideas and information. However, academic language is not the only factor that impacts oral language development.

Shusterman (2004) provides a wonderful example of dialectic differences in speech. Oral language is not just one entity. When addressing oral language, there are so many factors that we need to consider: dialect, idioms, slang, social language, and academic language are just a few of the factors that impact oral expression. In our classrooms, we work to move our students along the oral language continuum from only being comfortable using social language to developing fluency using academic discourse. Students need to understand their purpose for speaking, the audience to whom or with whom they are speaking, and the expectations for the many different forums and situations in which they are expected to speak. Antsy, the amusing protagonist from Shusterman's (2004) *The Schwa Was Here*, demonstrates in the previous excerpt how dialect can impact a student's oral language.

Oral language is a fundamental element of literacy and tends to develop along a typical continuum from preproduction to advanced fluency. There is a progression through the stages, even though all children do not reach the language milestones at exactly the same age. Usually, by about a year old, most children are able to understand about fifty words, vocalize about three words, and follow simple commands. The next year and a half is frequently a time of significant language growth. By two and a half, children can generally understand about 900 words and speak more than 570 words. By the beginning of kindergarten, children can typically comprehend about 4,000 words, understand the basic grammar rules of the language, and follow multistep directions (Loop, 2014).

Development along this five-stage continuum of preproduction, early production, emergent speech, developing fluency, and advanced fluency is impacted by the child's understanding of the four main aspects of the language system: phonology, semantics, syntax, and pragmatics (Van Zon, n.d.). Phonology encompasses the speech sounds and the rules for sequencing and combining these sounds. The ability to distinguish and understand the relationship between sounds is an important component in phonological awareness. Phonological awareness is one of the beginning reading skills.

Semantics involves the understanding of individual words and the combination of words into meaningful phrases or sentences. Semantics is broader than just the specific definition of the word in isolation. It also involves the understanding of the way the word is used in context. Consider the following two sentences: "After I heard the joke, I died laughing" and "After a long illness, my uncle died." The meaning of the word "died" is very different in each sentence, even though the word itself is used as a verb in each sentence.

Syntax involves understanding the relationship between the words within the sentence and how those words are combined to form larger units of phrases, clauses, and sentences (Van Zon, n.d.). This relationship is frequently evidenced in the subject–verb or the verb–direct object agreement (Bender, 2010). A child who has difficulty understanding or expressing sentences orally is likely to have the same difficulty when attempting to read or compose these written sentence forms. An understanding of morphology is an important aspect of syntax. Words can be composed of either bound or free morphemes. The word "cat" is just one morpheme or unit of meaning. However, the word "cats" contains two morphemes, "cat" and "s." Both morphemes, or word parts, carry meaning. "Cat" describes a four-legged creature with fur, while "s" indicates that there is more than one cat. "Cat" would be a free morpheme because it can stand alone, while "s" would be a bound morpheme, a morpheme that can only be used as a part of a larger word.

Morphology refers to the understanding of word parts and their meanings. The meaning of words can be changed by adding bound morphemes or affixes, whether they be prefixes or suffixes. For example, a suffix such as "ed" or "ing" can be added to the morpheme "camp," which would result in the tense of camp being changed from the present tense to the past (camped) or the present progressive tense (camping).

Pragmatics refers to the child's understanding of different ways to use language for a variety of purposes (Van Zon, n.d.). It could refer to the social or academic use of language. Pragmatics involves three major communication skills. The first skill is the ability to use language for different purposes. These purposes could include greeting, informing, demanding, promising, or requesting. The second skill would be the ability to change or adjust language usage based on the listener or the situation. These situations would include talking differently to an adult than the speaker does to a baby, providing an unfamiliar listener with additional information, and using different speech patterns in the classroom than on the playground. The final communication skill category would be the ability to follow rules for conversation and storytelling. This skill would include taking turns in conversations; introducing and staying on the topic; rephrasing to clarify misunderstandings; using verbal and nonverbal signals, facial expressions, and eye contact; and standing at acceptable distances in various situations. Rules in the pragmatic area vary from culture to culture (American Speech-Language-Hearing Association, 2014).

The four main aspects of the language system—phonology, semantics, syntax, and pragmatics—continue to develop throughout each of the five stages of the oral language continuum. Whether children are native speakers or English language learners (ELLs), they tend to progress through each of these stages. However, the amount of time children spend in each stage will differ depending upon their language background and exposure to the world. The preproduction stage is the time when learners are silent but are listening to the capable language users around them. During this time, they are learning the vocabulary and structure of the language. The early production stage typically lasts about a year while the learner is using single words or short phrases. In the emergent speech stage, learners are able to use simple sentences and construct short narratives. Developing fluency occurs when learners are able to use longer narratives and participate in conversations. During this stage, they are also demonstrating competency with beginning reading and writing; however, these ideas can often be expressed using inventive spellings. During the advanced fluency stage, learners perform as fluent speakers and writers and are able to use standard conventions in speaking, reading, and writing (Reutzel & Cooter, 2011).

LANGUAGE DIFFICULTIES

The development of reading and writing skills can be impacted by language deficits (Snow, Scarborough, & Burns, 1999). Oral language development deficits can be evidenced by a limited vocabulary, frequent use of nonspecific words such as "thing" and "stuff," limited use of complex sentences, and little use of description or elaboration (Greenhalgh & Strong, 2001). Lyons (1999) clearly describes the relationship between oral language and reading by indicating that proficient readers can use their "strong vocabularies and good syntactic and grammatical skills" (p. 10) to enhance the reading comprehension process.

Oral language development is impacted by many factors: physiological, social, environmental, and educational. Physiological issues that can impact oral language development include but are not limited to hearing loss, speech production issues, cleft lip and/or palate, traumatic brain injury, autism, and attention deficit hyperactivity disorder, to name just a few (Loop, 2014). These oral language issues could be evidenced through limited speech, poor vocabulary development, or difficulty with expressing needs or wants. Social factors, such as the amount and types of language interactions in the home, can also impact vocabulary development. From birth, children are absorbing the language they hear from their mom, dad, siblings, and caregivers, as well as those significant others around them. Not surprisingly, children are not only absorbing the spoken language but also forming meaning based upon the intonation used.

Environmental and socioeconomic factors can also impact language development. Hart and Risley (2002) recorded the words used in forty-two families over a two-and-a-half-year period. Families were categorized by income as professional, working class, or welfare level. The results of their study showed that children from the professional families were exposed to about 42 million words, children from working-class families were exposed to about 26 million words, while children from welfare families were exposed to only about 13 million words over the two-and-a-half-year time period. However, the number of words was not the only difference. The researchers also determined that the purpose for which the language was used was different. In professional families, the language emphasis was more on symbols and problem solving, and they demonstrated a greater use of nouns, modifiers, and past tense verbs. In contrast, in the welfare families there was greater emphasis on using language to teach socially acceptable behavior.

The study also indicated that professional families typically spent about forty minutes daily interacting with their young children, while welfare families spent approximately fifteen minutes daily. This difference was particularly evident in the frequency of interactions per hour. Professional families responded to their children about 250 times per hour (about 4 times a minute), while welfare families responded about 50 times per hour (approximately 1 time per minute). The use of language to express parental approval and encouragement was another area where differences were evident. In professional families this occurred about forty times per hour, but in welfare families only about four times per hour. The amount of conversation in the home was also significantly different. Professional families tended to converse using about 3,000 words per hour, while welfare families tended to speak about 500 words per hour. These differences resulted in a significant difference in language exposure, hence impacting the child's language development.

Finally, the educational environment is particularly important in helping to enhance the home language environment. These educational language opportunities can be provided through such activities as teacher talk, circle time, read alouds, shared reading, and partner talk. Teachers can encourage students' language development through informal and guided conversations that involve asking questions and providing time for students' explanations of their thinking or learning. Teachers should provide opportunities for students to discuss a wide range of topics through open-ended questioning and should encourage student talk about a variety of familiar topics. Teachers can also model and discuss vocabulary and formal English grammar while reading, writing, and sharing experiences (Annenberg Learner, 2002). In addition, teachers help to develop written and oral expression through "modeling, eliciting, probing, restating, clarifying, questioning, and praising" (Reutzel & Cooter, 2011, p. 70) students in oral conversation and written responses.

It is important to note that providing opportunities for oral language development is as important for students who live in low socio-economic areas, as it is for ELLs and students with speech and language disabilities. All of these groups of students frequently show language deficits in their written and oral discourse patterns. Being economically disadvantaged does not cause delayed language development; however, issues such as limited access to health care, lower parental education, and caregivers' limited educational levels can impact language development (Roseberry-McKibbin, 2012). Children with oral language deficits or delays frequently experience reading comprehension problems. These comprehension challenges are often associated with difficulties with vocabulary, grammar, and text level processing abilities (Mossberg-Michael, 2011).

ASSESSING ORAL LANGUAGE

Oral language assessment can occur formally or informally. Within the classroom, oral language assessment tends to occur more frequently using informal assessments or rating scales than as a formal test with a set of structured tasks administered using a standardized format. Informal language assessments, rather than measuring language use in isolation, allow the teacher to assess the student's spontaneous language usage in everyday speech. The freedom to express ideas in an individualistic way allows the teacher to develop a greater understanding of the "quantity and quality of the child's real oral language abilities" (Melear, 1974, p. 508).

Informal Assessment

An informal language inventory is easy to administer because it requires only one or two pictures and an audio recorder. The student is asked to tell the teacher about the pictures, and the teacher records the responses. After the recorded session, a predetermined amount of the recording is transcribed and analyzed. The number of sentences, grammatically correct sentences, describing terms, modifying phrases, morphemes, and mazes are recorded. Mazes would include such expressions as "uh," "mmm," "you know," and "like." This simple assessment is an easy way to document growth over time. However, the assessor should use the same time limit and similar pictures during each assessment period. Generally, time limits should be between two and five minutes. By limiting responses to a certain amount of time, scores between assessments can be compared to help determine the student's progress along the five-stage continuum from preproduction to advanced fluency. A chart such as the one in table 2.1 might be helpful for recording your results so that you can more easily track the student's progress over time.

SOLOM

The Student Oral Language Observation Matrix (SOLOM), rather than focusing on the fluency of production of each type of structure, gathers information about five different categories of language: comprehension, fluency, vocabulary, pronunciation, and grammar. For this assessment, possible five-point scores are calculated for each of the domains or categories. These can be

Table 2.1   Informal Oral Language Data Collection Chart

Date	# of Sentences	# of Correct Sentences	# of Descriptive Terms	# of Modifying Phrases	# of Morphemes	# of Mazes
xx/xx/xxxx						
xx/xx/xxxx						
xx/xx/xxxx						

combined to form a single total oral language score. This rating scale can be used to track progress over time in each of the domains or in total oral language. The SOLOM is not commercially published and is currently in public domain so it can be copied, modified, or adapted to meet individual needs. It was originally developed by the San Jose Area Bilingual Consortium. It can be used with second language learners or native English speakers (SOLOM, n.d.). After listening to the student's speech, the teacher places an *x* in the appropriate box in each domain, and then the totals are combined to form the total oral language score (see table 2.2).

The California State Department of Education (n.d.) has used this rating scale to identify four stages of oral language development. Stage 1 is Nonproficient in English, where the student has earned a total score of less than twelve points. Stage 2 is Emergent Limited English Proficiency where the student's total points on the rubric range from 12 to 18. Stage 3 is Developing Limited English Proficiency where the student's total score ranges between 19 and 24 points. Stage 4 is Fully English Proficient and would be a score of 25.

LANGUAGE ORGANIZES THOUGHT

Vygotsky (1978) posited that language is foundational for cognitive development. Language is a tool for developing "how" to think. Children learn about complex ideas through words as they internally process their external experiences. Speech and language are the major tools used to promote learning and to communicate with others. Spoken language is the foundation for reading and writing. Spoken language instruction facilitates writing growth, and writing instruction facilitates language growth (Mosburg-Michael, 2011). Of particular interest is Mosburg-Michael's (2011) observation that there is a direct relationship between students' academic achievement and the quantity and quality of talk occurring in the classroom. She indicated the importance of classroom discussion because there was a direct relationship between the quantity and quality of classroom talk and the academic achievement students demonstrated. Classrooms that had the highest quality of talk had the highest level of academic achievement. She found that high-performing students used metacognitive language tools to express their ideas more clearly. Therefore,

Table 2.2 Student Oral Language Observation Matrix (SOLOM)

	1	2	3	4	5
Comprehension	Cannot understand simple sentences.	Only understands conversational language spoken slowly.	Understands most of what is said at slower-than-normal speed with repetitions.	Understands most of what is said at slower-than-normal speed without repetition.	Understands everyday conversation and normal classroom discussions.
Fluency	Speech halting and fragmentary. Conversation virtually impossible.	Usually hesitant. Often forced into silence by language limitations.	Speech in everyday conversation and classroom discussion frequently disrupted by searching for the correct manner of expression.	Speech in everyday conversation and classroom discussions generally fluent, with occasional lapses while searching for the correct manner of expression.	Speech in everyday conversation and classroom discussions fluent and effortless. Approximating the speech of a native speaker.
Vocabulary	Vocabulary limitations so extreme as to make conversation virtually impossible.	Misuse and/or very limited word choice. Difficult to comprehend.	Student frequently uses wrong words. Conversation somewhat limited because of inadequate vocabulary.	Student occasionally uses inappropriate terms and/or must rephrase ideas because of lexical inadequacies.	Use of vocabulary and idioms approximates that of a native speaker.

Pronunciation	Pronunciation problems so severe as to make speech virtually unintelligible.	Very hard to understand because of pronunciation problems. Must frequently repeat in order to be understood.	Pronunciation problems necessitate concentration on the part of the listener and occasionally lead to misunderstanding.	Always intelligible, although the listener is conscious of a definite accent and occasional inappropriate intonation patterns.	Pronunciation and intonation approximate those of a native speaker.
Grammar	Errors in grammar and word order so severe as to make speech virtually unintelligible.	Grammar and word order errors make comprehension difficult. Must often rephrase and is restricted to basic patterns.	Frequent errors of grammar and/or word order occasionally obscure meaning.	Occasionally makes grammatical and/or word order errors that do not obscure meaning.	Grammar and word order approximate that of a native speaker.

in order to help students reach their academic potential, teachers need to engage students in academic conversations around specific content and texts.

Frequently classroom talk has been limited to one student answering a specific question posed by the teacher as a means to check student understanding rather than using discussion as a method for developing oral language and thinking. Durkin (1978–1979) provided much of the foundational research on classroom talk. He found that teachers mainly use questioning to check for understanding. Cazden (1988) later identified that classroom questioning often follows an initiate–respond–evaluate cycle. In this type of interaction, only one student has an opportunity to respond. This cycle often does not require more than one-word responses, so as a result, it does not help to expand or develop thinking or language.

Consequently, the development of communication and discussion skills within the classroom is particularly important. Classrooms should be structured so that children are exposed to ideas and have opportunities to work with these ideas in content area conversations (Fisher, Frey, & Rothenberg, 2008). With the inclusion of speaking and listening standards, oral language has been brought back to the forefront of today's literacy instruction. The Common Core speaking and listening standards state that "students must have ample opportunities to take part in a variety of rich, structured conversations—as part of a whole class, in small groups, and with a partner. Being productive members of these conversations requires that students contribute accurate, relevant information; respond to and develop what others have said; make comparisons and contrasts; and analyze and synthesize a multitude of ideas in various domains" (2014a, para. 8). Whether teachers adhere to the Common Core Standards or standards specific to their state, the research is clear, academic talk is important to not just literacy development but also to deepening understanding of content in all subject areas.

Dallimore, Hertenstein, and Butler (2017) completed a study in which 246 students shared how class discussions impacted their learning. More than 70 percent of the students in the study reported a positive relationship between not just their contributions to an academic discussion and learning but to the input of other students' comments in the discussion to their learning as well. Additionally, many students in the study indicated that required participation in a discussion resulted in better preparation on their part, and the preparation in itself contributed to their increased learning. The study goes on to summarize five ways that participation in discussion enhances learning: increasing engagement, retaining information, confirming previously learned information, clarifying prior knowledge, and deepening understanding.

Classroom talk can be used to develop students' thinking (Fisher et al., 2008). Discussion can be the bridge between reading and writing, but it can also be the bridge between reading, writing, and thinking. Consider asking students an important question, having them discuss that question, and then put pen to paper to respond to that question. The discussion has given them the opportunity to think through and solidify their thoughts. Or, consider asking a question, having students write in response to the question, share their response with their peers and after discussion, revise and edit their writing or thinking. Learning is or should be a social process.

So what is the difference between social and academic language? Have you ever overheard students speaking fluently with their peers but find that those same students contribute very little to classroom discussions? According to Spivey (2012), social language is the language we use when speaking with family members and friends, and social language allows us to use slang. Most of our students, with the exclusion of some ELLs and some students with exceptionalities, are proficient with social language. Academic language involves the vocabulary we need to succeed in the classroom or workplace. We use academic language to understand complex ideas and concepts and to process higher-order thinking. It is the language of textbooks, tests, and instruction. Because academic language can be particularly difficult for ELLs, we need to consider cultural differences, cognates, and visual assistance when teaching them academic language. Academic language can be more challenging for all learners and it needs to be taught and practiced. Providing opportunity for academic discourse is important, but we must also provide instruction in the expanded use of classroom academic conversations. Teachers need to consider incorporating methods such as sentence starters, sentence combinations, graphic organizers, and modeling to enhance students' oral language. Additional activities can be found in the final section of this chapter.

K–12 LANGUAGE DEVELOPMENT

There are six anchor standards in the speaking and listening area. Three cover comprehension and collaborations, and three cover the presentation of knowledge and ideas. Each of these standards increases in difficulty through the K–12 levels. In the following paragraph, the first anchor standard is used to illustrate this progression.

The first anchor standard for speaking and listening states that students should "Prepare for and participate effectively in a range of conversations and collaborations with diverse partners, building on other's ideas and expressing their own clearly and persuasively" (2014a, para. 2). As you examine this standard and its extensions for each grade level, you will note that beginning as early as kindergarten, students are expected to be able to follow accepted rules for conversations. In first grade, they are expected to be able to expand on ideas by asking clarifying questions. By second grade, students should be able to participate in discussions in a respectful manner. Even in the early years, students need to be taught and provided opportunities to practice using appropriate discussion protocols.

For this same standard and its progression through the intermediate grades, students are expected to prepare for discussion by studying or reading required materials and to contribute to the discussion appropriately. They should be able to follow agreed-upon rules and assigned roles in discussions, to ask and respond to questions, to elaborate on the ideas of other group members, and to note key ideas and draw conclusions as a result of their discussion.

In addition to all of the expectations from previous grades, students in the middle grades (six to eight) are expected to be able to provide evidence on the topic, text, or issue being discussed. By the middle grades, students should require only minimal supervision and be able to share in the responsibility for the discussion while tracking their own progress toward the goal or purpose of the discussion. Middle school students are expected to be able to use evidence to modify and justify their point of view on the topic.

By high school, students are expected to work together following set rules for decision-making and discussions, connect the discussion to bigger ideas related to the topic, summarize points of agreement or disagreement, probe the reasoning or evidence used in the discussion, hear and consider all positions on the topic, synthesize the information, and resolve contradictions to determine what further information is needed to deepen their understanding.

Although not all of the increasing expectations were noted in the progression analysis of this standard, it is evident that expectations for students' participation in collaborative discussions are specific and increasingly more difficult at each grade level. This speaking continuum begins in kindergarten with simple rules for discussions, such as listening to others and taking turns speaking. These desired oral language skills need to be taught through direct instruction, modeling, and practice. As teachers, we need to consider the best methods for helping students acquire oral language skills.

ORAL LANGUAGE ACTIVITIES

Telephone Game

Divide students into groups of five or six. Have students number off, and hand the first student in each group a word or a picture of a word. The words could be vocabulary from a current instructional unit. The student should not tell this word to anyone else until play begins. The first person whispers the name of the object to the second person, then the second person whispers the word to the third person; play continues until the word is whispered to the last person in the group. The final participant then whispers or writes the word for the teacher. The teacher has one student identify the word for the class. Each team that correctly identified the word gets a point. A new word is given to the second person, and the procedure is repeated. Awarding an extra credit point to each group that can define the word as well as identify it can extend the level of challenge in the game. To increase the level of difficulty even more, students could earn a bonus point by using the word appropriately in a sentence.

Book Talks

The purpose of a book talk is to "sell" the book so others are interested in reading it. The teacher might begin by modeling a book talk by giving some details about the book's characters, setting, or plot without giving away the whole book. The talk could also include excerpts from the book. Ending the book talk with a cliffhanger leaves the students wanting to read more!

Then make a copy of the book cover or jacket and post it on a bulletin board with a sign-out sheet. Students can sign out the book or add their name to the waiting list. After modeling the book talk, provide a calendar for students to sign up to give a book talk on a book that they are reading. Encourage students to follow your example. Provide them with a checklist or rubric to use as they prepare their book talk. A possible checklist follows:

1. My opening grabs the reader.
2. I include the title, author, and genre.
3. I describe the setting and characters.
4. I describe a portion of the plot.
5. I select an engaging excerpt to read aloud.
6. I speak clearly and with appropriate speed.
7. I speak loud enough to be heard in the back of the room.
8. My presentation is organized, and I am well prepared.
9. I read and enunciate clearly and with expression.
10. I make eye contact with the audience.

Text Detectives

From a text your class is about to read, select ten to fifteen interesting sentence-length quotes. Type these onto a sheet of paper leaving space between each quote. Cut the quotes apart so that there is one quote on each strip of paper. Duplicate as needed so that you have one sentence strip for each member of the class.

Divide the class into assigned discussion groups of four to five students. Write the group members' names on the board so that the students are aware of the group to which they will be returning after discussing with others. Set a timer for five minutes and allow students to mill about the room sharing their sentences with members of their own and other groups. The rules are simple. Students may speak to only one student at a time. They may read their sentence strip aloud to only the other person. No other discussion is allowed.

After the time is up, students go to their discussion groups and together write a collaborative prediction about the text based upon the sentence clues they have collected. Groups then share their predictions with the whole class. As a ticket out the door after reading the passage, students revise their predictions so that there are accurate statements about the text.

Jigsaw

Select an informational text that can logically be divided into several equal sections. Divide your students into the same number of groups as there are sections in the text. Assign one of these sections of the text to each group. This group will become the content experts for that portion of the text.

Allow the groups time to read the segments individually or with a partner. After reading the text segment, provide time for the groups to meet and determine how they will present the information from the text to others. Include time for the groups to rehearse their presentation.

Form new groups. Each group should contain at least one person from each of the expert groups. Each person in the new group gives their expert presentation to the newly formed group until all sections of the text have been presented. The group creates a summary synthesizing the information collected from each of the text sections.

Rate the Characters

Along the top of a large sheet of chart paper, write the names of the major characters from a narrative text that the class has read. Give each student one yellow and one blue sticky note and a black marker. On the yellow sticky note, each student writes the name of the character they feel is most important or has the most impact on the plot. Each student then writes the name of the second most important character on the blue sticky note.

The teacher then balances the groups by dividing the students based upon the character they chose as most important or second most important. Each group identifies specific sections of the text to support their character choice, organizes their ideas, and puts together a presentation supporting their position. The groups share their presentations with the class.

Reporter

After a unit has been taught on a controversial topic, as a class create a list of questions on the topic that can be used for an interview. The class is broken into pairs. One student is the expert on one side of the issue, and the other is the expert on the other side.

From each pair of students, one person is the interviewer and the other is the interviewee. The interviewer asks the questions and is responsible for understanding and appreciating the interviewee's perspective. Then the partners switch roles and repeat the process.

The students who interviewed a person representing the same perspective form a new group. They decide how to positively present to the class the perspective of the persons they interviewed. Each student must have a speaking portion in the presentation. When the process is complete, there will be two presentations, one representing each viewpoint.

Brain Dump

This activity can be used as an activating strategy to build background knowledge or as a summarizing strategy to review information. Divide the class into pairs. Students may decide who is going first. The first person is given two minutes to share everything he knows about the topic. After two minutes, the partners switch roles and the second person shares everything he knows about the topic for two minutes. It is acceptable to repeat some of the previous information. After four minutes, have each group share two interesting observations from their exchange.

Say It Another Way

This activity can be done with pairs of students or as a whole class. Students will get more practice when working in pairs, but responses can be more closely monitored during a whole-class activity. The first student makes a statement about the text you are reading or the topic or unit you are studying. The second student must paraphrase the first student's statement. When students are proficient with this activity, increase the difficulty by having the first student talk for one minute and then having the second student paraphrase the longer section.

This activity requires the students to listen to the speaker, identify the main topic and supporting details, and rephrase it.

Read Aloud

Read alouds are a great activity for any age level. They allow students to experience text that may be beyond their independent reading level. Read alouds provide models of appropriate English usage and expose students to more advanced vocabulary and sentence constructions while building content knowledge. In addition to listening to the text, students should be asked to summarize, synthesize, and comment on the passage. Make sure to pause during the reading to discuss the information presented. This activity provides opportunities for students to further explore content and to practice expressing their ideas clearly.

Toe the Line

Place a piece of masking tape on the classroom floor in the center of the room. Students stand about two steps away from the tape on either side. The teacher makes a statement about a controversial topic of study. Students are to take one step forward if they agree or one step backward if they disagree. Students can be randomly selected to share aloud their position and thinking. The activity continues as the teacher makes additional statements about the topic of study.

What's Missing?

Choose an ad from a newspaper or magazine. Omit one important piece of information from the ad and see who can find what other information is needed. The missing information could be price, telephone number, time, and so on.

What Did They Say?

Cut out pictures of groups of people. Each student chooses one picture. Using the facial expressions and other information within the picture, the student must create a logical conversation that could be occurring between the people in the group. After the conversations are written, all of the pictures are displayed in the front of the room. If the conversation is matched with the correct picture the child who wrote the conversation and the child who picked the correct picture each get a point. The student with the most points after all conversations are read wins. A revision of this could be that the student needs to create a conversation the group would logically have about the topic being studied based upon the information in the picture from the textbook or content text. The student needs to identify the pictorial support for why the person in the picture would say this. This revision requires the student to use the academic vocabulary in context.

Idiom Match

Upper elementary and middle through high school students are developing their understanding of figurative language. Using a deck of blank cards, write an idiom on one card. Then write its meaning on a different card. Students match the idiom to its meaning and use the idiom in a sentence. This game can be played like either Memory or Fish.

Socratic Seminar

Socratic Seminar is a formal academic discussion. The teacher chooses the text(s) and topic. Students closely read the texts numbering the paragraphs, underlining important information, and creating critical questions or making comments to deepen their understanding of the topic/text in the margins. Socratic Seminar generally takes place in a large circle, but alternative formats can be effective. Remind students that Socratic Seminar is used to deepen their understanding of a topic or text. It is not a debate or an argument. The teacher generally begins with a central question and throughout the seminar students are encouraged to ask questions to deepen their understanding. The teacher may need to prompt students or ask additional questions to move the seminar forward. Questions should allow students to probe deeper, clarify understanding, paraphrase and add on, or synthesize the information (Davenport, 2016). Hands are not raised in a seminar, but respectful, inclusive discourse is encouraged. Students should reference the text(s) throughout the discussion. At the conclusion of the seminar, allow time for students to reflect on their participation in this oral language experience and set goals for increased or improved participation in future seminars.

Philosophical Chairs

Teacher presents a controversial statement to the class. Students spend a few minutes writing their thinking about the topic. The teacher designates a place in the room for students in agreement with the statement, students in disagreement with the statement, and for those who are undecided. One student kicks off the discussion by stating his opinion and why, referencing a text if one has been used. A student from the opposing side of the room restates what the first student said and respectfully states reasons for disagreement. This process continues; however, the teacher periodically stops the discussion to see if anyone has been convinced to change sides or if those who are undecided have chosen a side. The students move to the side with which they are in agreement and the discussion continues until the teacher calls an end to it. Take some time to reflect on the discussion. Ask students to recognize what may have prompted them to change their thinking, why they did not change their thinking, or if the discussion has caused them to be undecided on the topic (Fletcher, 2019).

REFERENCES

American Speech-Language-Hearing Association. (2014). Social language use. Retrieved from http://www.asha.org/public/speech/development/Pragmatics/.

Annenberg Learner. (2002). Essential components of literacy development. Retrieved from http://www.learner.org/libraries/readingk2/front/components.html.

Bender, W. N. (2010). Syntax and semantics. Retrieved from http://www.education.com/reference/article/syntax-semantics/.

California State Department of Education. (n.d.). *Student Oral Language Observation Matrix.* Retrieved from http://www.cal.org/twi/evaltoolkit/appendix/solom.pdf.

Cazden, C. B. (1988). *Classroom Discourse: The Language of Teaching and Learning.* Portsmouth, NH: Heinemann.

Common Core State Standards Initiative. (2014a). *English Language Arts Standards: Anchor Standards: College and Career Readiness Anchor Standards for Speaking and Listening.* Retrieved from http://www.corestandards.org/ELA-Literacy/CCRA/SL/.

Dallimore, E. J., Hertenstein, J. H., & Platt, M. B. (2017, March). How do students learn from participation in class discussion? *Faculty Focus: Higher Ed Teaching Strategies from Magna Publications.* Retrieved from https://www.facultyfocus.com/articles/effective-teaching-strategies/students-learn-participation-class-discussion/.

Davenport, M. (2016, September). Socratic seminars: Building a culture of student-led discussion. *Edutopia.* Retrieved from http://edutopia.org/blog/socratic-seminars-culture-student-led-discussion-mary-davenport.

Durkin, D. (1978–1979). What classroom observations reveal about reading comprehension instruction. *Reading Research Quarterly, 14,* 481–533.

Finley, T. (2014, January 2). 8 strategies for teaching academic language. Retrieved from https://www.edutopia.org/blog/8-strategies-teaching-academic-language-todd-finley.

Fisher, D., Frey, N., & Rothenberg, C. (2008). *Content Area Conversations: How to Plan Discussion-based Lessons for Diverse Language Learners.* Alexandria, VA: ASCD.

Fletcher, J. (2019, May). A framework for whole class discussions. *Edutopia.* Retrieved from https://edutopia.org/article/framework-whole-class-discussions.

Greenhalgh, K. S., & Strong, C. J. (2001). Literate language features in spoken narratives of children with typical language and children with language impairments. *Language, Speech, & Hearing Services in Schools, 32*(2), 114–126.

Hart, B., & Risley, T. R. (1995). *Meaningful Differences in the Everyday Experiences of Young American Children.* Baltimore, MD: Paul H. Brookes.

Loop, E. (2014). Factors influencing a child's language development. *Global Post Every Day Life.* Retrieved from http://everydaylife.globalpost.com/factors-influencing-childs-language-development-6487.html.

Lyons, G. R. (1999). Reading development, reading disorders, and reading instruction: Research-based findings. *Language Learning and Education* [ASHA Special Interest Division 1 Newsletter], *6*(1), 8–16.

Melear, J. D. (1974). An informal language inventory. *Elementary English, 51*(4), 508–531. Retrieved from http://www.jstor.org/discover/10.2307/41387238?uid=3739600&uid=2129&uid=2&uid=70&uid=4&uid=3739256&sid=21103764611057.

Mosburg-Michael, S. (2011). Supporting vocabulary and language development through collaboration with classroom teachers. Retrieved from file:///E:/Rowman%20and%20Littlefield/Mosburg-Michael.pdf.

Reutzel, D. R., & Cooter, R. B. (2011). *Strategies for Reading Assessment and Instruction: Helping Every Child Succeed* (4th ed.). Boston: Pearson.

Roseberry-McKibbin, C. (2012). The impact of poverty and homelessness on children's oral and literate language: Practical implications for service delivery. Retrieved from https://www.asha.org/uploadedFiles/Poverty-Homelessness-Childrens-Oral-Literate-Language.pdf.

Schusterman, N. (2004). *The Schwa Was Here.* New York: Scholastic.

Snow, C. E., Scarborough, H. S., & Burns, M. S. (1999). What speech-language pathologists need to know about early reading. *Topics in Language Disorders, 20*(1), 48–58.

SOLOM. (n.d.). Student oral language observation matrix. Retrieved from http://www.cal.org/twi/evaltoolkit/appendix/solom.pdf.

Spivey, B. L. (2019). Social and academic vocabulary – what's the difference? *Handy Handouts, 365.* Retrieved from https://www.handyhandouts.com/pdf/365%20Social%20&%20Acad%20vocab.pdf.

Van Zon, L. (n.d.). Exploring the connection between oral language and literacy. *Exceptional Learning Centre.* Retrieved from http://exlcentre.com/wp-content/uploads/2012/04/ExploringConnections.pdf.

Vygotsky, L. (1978). *Readings on the Development of Children,* ed. Mary Gauvain and Michael Cole. Retrieved from http://www.psy.cmu.edu/~siegler/vygotsky78.pdf.

Chapter 3

Phonological Awareness

CLASSROOM VISIT

Journal Entry

Febuary 10

I offen go the libery by my houz with my mom on Wednesdays. Last week I was working on a projik for histry. We are studying the goverment. I was asked to do the part about the "candidates in the last election for president." So I was working in the back corner of the libery when a spiter suddley crawled up from under the table and was walking acrost mypin. Now I'm not especially scart of spiters but this was a big one.

I yelled and everyone in the place looked at me. I was thinking about crawling under the table when the liberryan walked over to me, looked down at the spiter and with out a word picked it up by a leg and gintly set it outside the window. She looked at me and smiled and said, "Don't be scart of them. They're not dangerous."

I hate spiters. I'm not scart of them. I jist hate them.

Mrs. Smith had begun incorporating writing journals into her daily classroom routine immediately following the winter holiday break. Every Friday she collected the journals, read students entries, and commented in them. This was a great opportunity for her to learn more about her students, to show students the fun of communicating through writing, and most importantly to monitor their learning. In the almost two months of journal entries, she had seen vast growth in her students' abilities to express themselves in writing.

41

Table 3.1 Error Analysis of Christine's Journal Entry

Misspelled Word	Actual Word	Initial Error	Medial Error	Final Error	Notes
offen/spiter/ scart/acrost	often/spider/ scared/across		x	x	Difficulty with /t/ and /d/
liberry/Febuary	library/February		x		Difficulty with /r/
projik/jist/pin	project/just/pen		x		Short vowel confusion: /i/, /u/, /e/
houz	house			x	Confusion: /s/ and /z/
histry/suddley	history/suddenly		x		Missing center syllable
goverment	government		x		Missing /n/

This Friday afternoon, she paused looking at Christine's journal entry. Christine was a bright student with great ideas that were generally well developed, but Ms. Smith was noticing a pattern in Christine's writing that indicated she might be having difficulty hearing the individual sounds, or phonemes in words she was using in her writing. Clearly Christine understood the meaning of the words since she was using them correctly, but her misspellings were numerous. More importantly, a pattern in her errors was becoming evident. Most, if not all, of her misspellings involved specific phonemes.

When Mrs. Smith thought back to Christine's speech, she realized that Christine did not always enunciate clearly; the encoding errors in her journal were not a surprise. She decided to take the time to do an error analysis of Christine's journal entry (see table 3.1) to determine what specific areas she should address during instruction.

Looking back at the errors in this most recent journal entry, it was clear that initial sounds in words were not an issue for Christine. She demonstrated a strong understanding of the sound–symbol relationship in the initial position. However, medial errors were common. Christine seemed to often omit medial sounds in words. This was the most frequent type of error. The specific sounds /r/, /t/, /d/, and /n/ were frequently omitted. In the medial position, the short vowel sounds for /i/, /e/, and /u/ were also confused. Difficulty with final sounds was not as frequent. However, the /ng/ sound was omitted twice in the final position. Christine also demonstrated some difficulty distinguishing between the /s/ and /z/ sounds.

The error analysis confirmed what Mrs. Smith was seeing Christine do in other situations. When writing, Christine often uses the vowel "i" for words that actually contain the short /ĕ/ and /ŭ/ sounds. Providing encoding instruction with the short /i/ vowel sound could have a positive impact on her correct usage of other short vowel sounds.

Mrs. Smith made a plan to also focus on having Christine orally repeat vocabulary with an emphasis on the medial phonemes and syllables because Christine was often missing these syllables in her writing. When repeating vocabulary, helping Christine count the number of times her jaw drops with each word would help her know how many syllables should be in the word. Each syllable contains one vowel sound, so this would provide information about the number of vowel sounds to encode in the word. This would help her to make sure she encodes all the vowel sounds when she writes.

LITERARY CONNECTION

Allowing time for practice of the spoken word is a strategy that can positively impact students' encoding and decoding of the written word. Word play is a great way to help develop phonological awareness, whether the student is in kindergarten or middle school. Many picture books such as Dr. Seuss's and poetry such as Shel Silverstein's are wonderful resources because they appeal to a wide range of ages. Phonological awareness can be developed through rhyme, alliteration, assonance, consonance, onomatopoeia, tongue twisters, jump rope rhymes, songs, and raps. These are just a few ways to have fun with words. Here is an example of a tongue twister using alliteration:

Chester chooses chestnuts, cheddar cheese with chewy chives. He chews them and he chooses them. He chooses them and he chews them . . . those chestnuts, cheddar cheese and chives in cheery, charming chunks. (Freed, 1952)

Shel Silverstein's *Runny Babbit* is full of excellent examples of phoneme deletions and substitutions. Following is a short excerpt illustrating his clever manipulation of phonemes by exchanging the initial phoneme of one word with the initial phoneme of another word in the same line:

Way down in the green woods
Where the animals all play,
They do things and they say things

In a different sort of way—
Instead of sayin' "purple hat,"
They all say "hurple pat."
Instead of sayin' "feed the cat,"
They just say "ceed the fat."
So if you say, "let's bead a rook
That's billy as can se,"
You're talkin' Runny Babbit talk,
Just like mim and he.
(Silverstein, 2005, p. 4)

WHAT IS PHONOLOGICAL AWARENESS?

Phonological awareness and phonemic awareness are often used interchange-ably, but there are slight differences in meaning. Phonological awareness is an understanding of all the sounds around us. This broad umbrella of auditory skills incorporates many components; word awareness, onset–rime aware-ness, syllable awareness, and phonemic awareness all fall under that umbrella (Lane, 2007). The Common Core State Standards (2014) broadly define phonological awareness as "the ability to demonstrate an understanding of spoken words, syllables, and sounds or phonemes." Phonological awareness includes the ability to identify and manipulate units of oral language such as words, syllables, and onsets and rimes (Reading Rockets, n.d). Phonological awareness provides the basis for developing an understanding of phonics. Phonics and phonological awareness are two more terms that are often con-fused because they are very similar. However, there is an easy way to tell the difference between the two. If you are describing activities that you could do with your eyes closed, you are probably working in the phonological strand only. If you need to open your eyes to complete the activity, you have prob-ably begun to incorporate some phonics activities as well.

Typically phonological awareness instruction occurs in kindergarten and first grade. This phonological instruction is important because it can help to improve both spelling and reading skills. Once students have mastered the phonological awareness strand, more instruction in phonological awareness is generally not needed. Typically, fifteen to twenty hours of phonological awareness instruction is sufficient for students to develop an understanding of the sound system (Lane, 2007). However, sometimes with older struggling readers or English language learners (ELLs), specific components or phonemes may need to be addressed.

Phonemic awareness also involves the ability to understand how sounds within a word operate. By definition, phonemic awareness specifically refers to the ability to "focus on and manipulate individual sounds (phonemes) in spoken words" (Reading Rockets, n.d., para. 1) and is purely an auditory skill. Phonemes are the smallest unit of a spoken language and can be combined in various ways to form syllables and words. Spoken English is comprised of forty-four phonemes. A single sound or phoneme may be represented by an individual letter (grapheme) or by a combination of letters. In English, a single letter may also be used to represent two different phonemes, such as "a" in both cap and cape. Or, a single phoneme may be represented in a number of different ways. For example, the phoneme /f/ can be represented by the letter or grapheme "f" or by the two-letter combination "ph." So even though we only have forty-four phonemes, there are significantly more ways to encode or represent those phonemes. Sousa (2005) indicated that this factor is part of what makes English difficult to learn. In his research, he compared the relationship between phonemes and the number of ways to spell the phonemes in a variety of languages. Italian had thirty-three phonemes and twenty-five ways to spell those sounds. Spanish had approximately thirty-five phonemes with thirty-eight ways to spell those sounds. However, English had 44 phonemes with more than 1,100 ways to spell those sounds. This fact can make English reading and writing difficult for students to master.

Phonemic awareness provides the foundation for spelling and word recognition skills. Proficiency with phonemic awareness is the best predictor of how well children will learn to read (Reading Rockets, n. d.). Lyon (1995) indicated that "phonemic awareness is the core and causal factor that separates normal readers from disabled readers." Struggling students do not seem to experience difficulty hearing the big chunks, words, and syllables. It is the sounds within the individual syllables that they experience difficulty discriminating. Consequently, the match between the sound–symbol relationship becomes difficult, and they often end up trying to memorize the word by its shape. This can be an effective strategy during the primary years, when many of the sight words are being introduced and the number of words is more limited. However, as the printed vocabulary expands to include many words with similar shapes, this method for identifying words becomes less effective. As a result, these struggling students tend to experience difficulty in reading comprehension by about fourth grade, not because they don't understand the concepts, but because they are having difficulty decoding the increased vocabulary expressed through the multisyllabic words that now compose about 70 percent of the text. As a result of this increase in the amount of multisyllabic words, comprehension difficulties seem to develop because the meaning of the text is carried by those longer words the struggling readers are having difficulty decoding. If the passage were read orally to these students, they would often be able to comprehend it. As a result, we can likely conclude that if students can comprehend a text that the teacher reads aloud to them, comprehension is not the issue. Listening to students read the text aloud could prove or disprove this assumption. If when reading the text aloud, students are struggling at the word level, this would confirm that decoding is an issue. There may be other issues, but decoding is an issue that needs to be addressed.

Phonemic awareness is the best predictor of who is going to experience difficulty in reading by fifth grade. Stanovich (1994) observed that phonemic awareness is more highly related to learning to read than intelligence or reading readiness. So the importance of developing effective phonemic awareness skills cannot be ignored. There are seven essential phonemic awareness skills that students need to have mastered: counting or saying each sound, adding a sound, deleting a sound, changing a sound, comparing two words, blending sounds into words, and creating words that rhyme.

Dechant (1993) examined these seven skills a little more extensively by dividing them into three levels. His first level of phonemic awareness moved from word awareness, to rhyme awareness, and finally to syllable awareness, segmentation, and blending. The second level included awareness of initial consonant sounds, alliteration, onset–rime segmentation, and blending. The third level encompassed phonemic segmentation, phonemic blending, and phonemic manipulation, including addition, deletion, and substitution of phonemes. Proficiency with all of these skills is essential for successfully mastering the reading process.

Teacher Knowledge Survey

Of course, as adult English speakers, we have already developed these phonological skills; consequently, these should not be difficult for us to teach.

Right? Just for fun, test your knowledge by attempting the following four questions from Moats' Teacher Knowledge Survey (2009). Take a minute to answer each question, and then check your answers. The percentage in parentheses after each answer is the percentage of primary grade teachers in her research sample who were able to answer the question correctly.

1. A syllable is: (50 percent)
    A. The same as a rime
    B. A unit of speech organized around a vowel sound
    C. A sequence of letters that includes one or more vowel letters
    D. Equivalent to a morpheme
2. How many spoken syllables are in each word?
    nationality (95 percent), enabling (48 percent), incredible (95 percent), shirt (87 percent), and cleaned (69 percent)
3. How many phonemes or distinct speech sounds are in each word?
    straight (33 percent), explain (1 percent), lodged (45 percent), know (68 percent), racing (13 percent), and eighth (75 percent)
4. Which word has a schwa? (55 percent)
    A. eagerly
    B. prevent
    C. definition
    D. formulate
    E. story

Answers

Now, check your answers. The correct answer is in italics.

1. A syllable is: (50 percent)
    A. The same as a rime
    B. *A unit of speech organized around a vowel sound*
    C. A sequence of letters that includes one or more vowel letters
    D. Equivalent to a morpheme
2. How many spoken syllables are in each word?
    nationality *(5)*, enabling *(3)*, incredible *(4)*, shirt *(1)*, and cleaned *(1)*
3. How many phonemes or distinct speech sounds are in each word?
    straight *(5)*, explain *(7)*, lodged *(4)*, know *(2)*, racing *(5)*, and eighth *(2)*

4. Which word has a schwa? (55 percent)
   A. eagerly
   B. prevent
   C. *definition*
   D. formulate
   E. story (Moats, 2009)

As you can see from the percentage correct in the first question, only about half of the primary teachers were able to identify the correct definition of a syllable. As teachers, we need to be aware that each syllable has only one vowel sound. The important distinction is not the number of vowels but the number of sounds those vowels make. This explains why "B" is the correct answer for the first question.

Auditory discrimination is a learned skill that is still developing as students begin their formal schooling experience. Some children can quickly understand the concept of syllables by clapping the parts they hear in words. Other children may have difficulty determining exactly what is meant by parts or syllables. They are probably hearing the sounds but have not determined exactly what they are supposed to be listening for. To scaffold instruction in syllable identification, have students place their hand under their chin. Then have the student say the word "outloud." As they say the word, they should count the number of times their chin drops. Each syllable is a "push of breath" (Barzilay, 2001, para. 3), so each time the push of breath is expelled, the chin drops. This additional tactile support may help your struggling students develop the auditory discrimination skills they need to be successful in identifying syllables within words.

In question 2, most teachers did not experience significant difficulty determining the number of syllables in the word. Only "enabling" and "cleaned" seemed to cause a little bit of confusion. "Enabling" has three vowel sounds (en-a-bling) because each vowel makes a separate sound. However, "cleaned," although it has three vowels, only has one vowel sound since the "a" is silent and makes the first "e" long, and the "ed" is pronounced as the /d/ sound. Since there is only one vowel sound, it is only a one-syllable word. If the ending had been pronounced as /id/, this sound would have added another syllable.

Generally, the teachers in the study found identifying the number of phonemes in a word to be more difficult. As we look back at the words in question 3, keep in mind that a phoneme is an individual speech sound. Each individual phoneme is written between two slanted lines. "Straight" has five sounds—/s/-/t/-/r/-/a/-/t/. The letters "i," "g," and "h" in this word are not pronounced, leaving only five phonemes. The word "explain" is tricky, as you can see, since only 1 percent of the primary teachers in the sample were able to identify the number of phonemes correctly. There are seven phonemes—/e/-/k/-/s/-/p/-/l/-/a/-/n/. In English, the letter "x" is actually produced by combining two phonemes, /k/ and /s/. The letter "x" does not have its own distinct sound. The word "lodged" has a silent "d," and the "ed" combination only makes one sound, /d/. "Lodged" has four phonemes—/l/-/o/-/g/-/d/. "Know" has only two sounds. Both the "k" and the "w" are silent; consequently the phonemes would be /n/-/o/. In the word "racing," the /ng/ combination only makes one sound even though it is represented by two letters, so the phonemes are /r/-/a/-/c/-/i/-/ng/. Finally, in the word "eighth," "eigh" makes a single long /a/ sound and "th" is a diphthong that makes one sound. This means that the phonemes in "eighth" would be /a/-/th/.

An understanding of phonemes is vital when teaching beginning reading. Teachers must have an understanding about how our sound system operates so they can help students take those individual phonemes and combine them to form words. This process of identifying phonemes and making a sound–symbol match is further complicated by the way in which the phonemes are produced. Some phonemes are stops while others are continuants. This is an important distinction for you as a teacher to understand. When producing some phonemes the air is stopped inside the mouth, while in others the air flows out without being stopped. For example, say the /s/ phoneme. Make sure that you don't add a vowel sound to the end. Then try the same thing with the /d/ phoneme. You will notice that the /s/ continues while the /d/ stops. When you are teaching your students to blend letters together to form words, it will be easier for them to begin by learning to blend those that are continuants rather than trying to blend stops (Clear English, n.d.). For example, it is easier for a student to begin by learning to blend the phonemes in "sat" than those in "cat."

In question 4, teachers who experienced difficulty did not know the sound associated with schwa. The English Plus website (2014) defines "schwa" as "the vowel sound in many lightly pronounced unaccented syllables in words of more than one syllable" (para. 1). The schwa is typically pronounced "uh." This is another reason, perhaps, why English is particularly confusing, because any of the vowels in English can be used to represent this sound. Examples of the schwa would include "the a in adept, the e in synthesis, the i in decimal, the o in harmony, the u in medium, and the y in syringe" (para. 2).

CONTINUUM OF PHONOLOGICAL AWARENESS

Phonological awareness is a learned skill. It tends to develop along a phonological continuum. Phonological awareness instruction typically begins in preschool and continues through kindergarten and/or first grade. Instruction typically begins with an understanding of rhyme and then moves to alliteration. As students' skills develop, they begin by distinguishing between the beginning and endings sounds of individual words. They then move to sentence segmentation. At this stage, they develop the ability to distinguish between words in a sentence. For example, you might see that students in the early stages of phonological awareness consider "I love you" to be one word because it is one thought. After they develop an understanding of words, phonological awareness skills continue to develop. Students soon begin to distinguish the individual syllables within the word. This is followed by the ability to separate between the onset and the rime within words. The onset is the beginning of a syllable up to the vowel, and the rime is the section from the vowel through the end of the syllable. In the word "cat," the onset is "c" and the rime is "at." In the word "strand," the onset is "str" and the rime is "and." This is often the type of instruction used when working with word families.

However, single-syllable words can be divided in another way as well. They can be separated into body and coda. Murray et al. (2008) suggest that children might more easily blend body and coda parts as opposed to onsets and rimes because when decoding using body and coda students move from left to right across the page rather than first focusing on the word family ending and then going back to the beginning of the word. When decoding using body and coda, the body would include the beginning of the word through the vowel sound, and the coda would be after the vowel to the end of the word. So, for the word "cat," the body would be "ca" and the coda would be "t." If students are experiencing difficulty blending and segmenting onset and rime, you might want to try providing instruction using body and coda.

The last developing phonological skill involves multiple steps. It is the ability to identify, segment, blend, and delete individual phonemes. For example, students might be asked to identify what word is formed when the /sk/ is removed from the word "skip" and an /h/ is added to the beginning of the remaining portion, or rime, of the word. If students identify the word "hip," it is evident that they have been able to hold onto the stimulus information, mentally manipulate the sounds, and replace them with the new information.

Auditory discrimination is also a learned skill. Of our forty-four phonemes, some have only minimal differences. These are generally the ones that students have the most difficulty discriminating between: /f/ and /v/, /t/ and /d/, /b/ and /d/, /i/ and /e/, and /o/ and /u/ (Hudson, 2005). Discrimination of these sounds will tend to develop more slowly and may require more instruction and practice. When students are experiencing difficulty, it might be helpful to also discuss how the sounds are physiologically produced so that learners can focus on the physical action as they make the sound, until they develop the auditory discrimination needed to distinguish the difference between similar phonemes. For example, when making the /v/ sound, the top teeth rest on the bottom lip and a vibration can be felt on the bottom lip. When making the /f/ sound, the top teeth also rest on the bottom lip but there is not a vibration.

Learning about the physiological production might also be particularly helpful when distinguishing between the five short vowel sounds. The short i, short o, and the short a are produced much higher in the throat then the short e or short u. The short e is produced in about the middle of the throat, and the short u is produced at the bottom of the throat. Having a student place his hand on his throat to feel where the vibrations occur might help him learn to identify the minimal differences in the vowel sounds.

University of Oregon (n.d.) has a wonderful visual illustrating the phonological continuum. You might want to check out their website. Their site also contains curriculum maps indicating the typical grade level for instruction in each of these skills. Phonological skills develop from the largest differences to the finer distinctions. The continuum of phonemic awareness development progresses from easy to more difficult. It begins with word comparison; moves to rhyming, sentence segmentation, syllable segmentation and blending, onset–rime blending and segmentation, and blending and segmenting individual phonemes; and ends with phoneme deletion and manipulation.

The Foundational Standards of the Common Core stress the importance of teaching rhyming, segmentation, blending, and manipulation of phonemes for beginning readers to help them develop an understanding of the sound–symbol relationship.

This particular strand is not as significant a concern once readers have a basic understanding of the sound–symbol relationship. However, as was evidenced in Christine's writing, there might be isolated phonemes that need to be addressed to help support the decoding and encoding process with some struggling readers or writers.

ASSESSMENTS

Since we previously examined the phonological continuum, we know that phonemic awareness encompasses many skills. Consequently, there really is not just one assessment that covers all aspects of this strand. Depending on where the student is on the continuum, you may be interested in assessing any one of Dechant's (1993) categories: word awareness, rhyming, syllable segmentation and blending, initial consonants, alliteration, onset–rime segmentation and blending, phonemic segmentation and blending, and phonemic manipulation, including addition, deletion, and substitution. Many assessments for analyzing these skills are available for free on the Internet.

However, the first step in mastering all of these skills is the development of auditory discrimination skills. Auditory discrimination assessments can be used to evaluate these skills. Wepman's Auditory Discrimination test, which was originally published in 1958 and revised in 1973, is probably the best known. The test consists of forty-word pairs and only requires five to ten minutes to administer. These word pairs are constructed so that there are minimal differences in only one of the initial (pin–tin), final (best–bet), or medial (pin–pen) phonemes. This assessment was normed based on a sample of 2,000 children (Alic, 2006).

Similar informal screening tools like the one in table 3.2 can be constructed to help determine the next steps in auditory discrimination instruction. Since these are informal, they are not normed but can provide helpful information for guiding instruction.

Additional informal assessments, such as the Staugler Literacy rubric (2007), can be used to progress monitor phonemic awareness, concepts of

Table 3.2 Same or Different Auditory Discrimination

Instructions for Administration

This phonological awareness assessment involves both word and sound
discrimination. Children are asked to determine if two words or sounds are the
same or different.

Introduce the Task

Have the student sit with his back to you so that decisions are made based upon
the auditory discrimination of the phonemes rather than visual cues you may
unconsciously provide. Tell the student, "I will say two words. Listen to the words
and tell me if the words are the same or different. For example, if I said cat-hug,
you would say the words were different. Now it is your turn. Let's try another. If
I said hat-hat, would you say the words are different or the same?" If the student
responds correctly and appears to understand the task, continue; if not, provide
some additional examples.

Scoring the Task

Three different sets of words are provided. Record a 1 on the line if the student
correctly determines if the set of words is the same or different. Record a 0 on
the line if the student answers incorrectly. Two words in each set are the same.
Discontinue testing if a student scores less than 70 percent correct in any set of
words.

Set 1: Word Level

___ baseball-basketball	___ sad-sad
___ race-rent	___ tack-slack
___ shoe-shark	___ feet-fine
___ hammer-hammock	___ window-wonder
___ tap-tap	___ shipwreck-battleship
___ vest-past	___ sap-slap

Total Correct ___/10

Set 2: Initial and Final Phonemes

___ pet-pen	final /t/-/n/	___ toad-load	initial /t/-/l/
___ tree-tree		___ dose-toes	initial /d/-/t/
___ van-fan	initial /v/-/f/	___ help-held	final /p/-/d/
___ yet-yes	final /t/-/s/	___ sip-zip	initial /s/-/z/
___ dog-dog		___ talk-walk	initial /t/-/w/

Total Correct ___/10

Set 3: Medial Position

___ donkey-dinky	/o/-/i/	___ table-tattle	/t/-/b/
___ wag-wig	/a/-/i/	___ cuddle-cuddle	
___ red-rid	/e/-/i/	___ apple-apple	
___ able-apple	/b/-/p/	___ bottle-battle	/o/-/a/
___ balloon-baboon	/l/-/b/	___ dog-dig	/o/-/i/
___ cattle-kettle	/a/-/e/	___ bean-bin	/ea/-/i/

Total Correct ___/10

print, word recognition, fluency, and reading comprehension. The student reads a short passage aloud to the teacher while the teacher evaluates the student's reading. Students earn a score between 1 and 5 in each category. The number of points earned are combined generating a total for the five categories. Based upon the number of points earned the student is classified as Early Emerging, Early Transitional Emerging, Transitional Emerging, Late Transitional Emerging, or Early Conventional. The information from the rubric can be used to guide instruction more specifically.

PHONOLOGICAL AWARENESS
AND OLDER STUDENTS

Phonological awareness is generally considered a skill for primary students; however, awareness of phonemes in words can be significant for older students as well. This can be evidenced in the pronunciation of everyday words. When listening to a class of students reciting the Pledge of Allegiance, have you ever heard any of the students pronouncing the word indivisible as invisible? Or, have you ever seen a student spell the word spider as spiter? If you listen carefully as students pronounce the word, spider, you will often hear the /d/ phoneme pronounced as a /t/, and this translates to their writing.

According to Moats and Tolman (2009), phonological instruction is relevant for older students who are "inattentive to the internal details of the spoken word" (para. 1). There are several strategies that support phonological awareness for older students. One strategy is to have students recognize whether words have been pronounced correctly. You might consider intentionally mispronouncing a vocabulary term in an effort to encourage them to catch the mispronunciation and correct it. Another strategy is to ask students to pronounce vocabulary terms aloud; this can be done independently or chorally. Also, you can point out similar sounding words, for example, entomologist, etymologist. Another effective strategy is to pronounce new vocabulary in syllable chunks and have students repeat the term as the full word. For example, the teacher says "in-di-vis-i-ble" and the students reply "indivisible." Student engagement will increase if you explain that you want the students to be comfortable using the terms in academic conversations. It is important that they learn to pronounce vocabulary terms properly to support academic conversations, as well as decoding and encoding skills.

PHONOLOGICAL AWARENESS AND ELLS

Earlier in this chapter we discussed that there are forty-four phonemes in the English language. When we consider our ELLs we must be aware that some of the phonemes of English may not be in their home language. It may be difficult for these students to pronounce and recognize the different English phonemes. Therefore, while teaching vocabulary, teachers also need to teach phonemic awareness (Antunez, 2002).

If ELLs have mastered the sounds of their home language, then they are more likely to master the sounds of English. If the teacher assesses the phonemes that the ELLs already have and can manipulate, then the teacher can focus on the sounds that are unfamiliar and need to be taught. ELLs will benefit from instruction in the phonemes of our language (Hagan, 2010).

PHONEMIC AWARENESS ACTIVITIES

Sound Counting (Elkonin Boxes)

You will need pictures of familiar objects and chips. Students are given a pile of chips. The teacher pronounces the word slowly, elongating each phoneme within the word, while students place a chip on the table to represent each sound they hear in the word. The teacher models saying each sound in the word. Students then follow the teacher's model and touch each chip as they say the sound it represents in the word. They then combine the sounds and pronounce the complete word.

Change or Take Away Game

The game focuses on the skill of consonant substitution. You will need a list of simple phrases where each word begins with the same letter and a set of twenty-one cards where each card has a single consonant written on it. The vowels are not included in this activity.

The teacher reads one of the phrases. The student picks one of the consonant cards. She must change the initial letter of each of the alliterative words in the sentence to match the letter on her card. The new phrase will be a silly, nonsense phrase. For example, the phrase on the teacher's card might read

"Larry's lizard leaps." If the student chooses the card with the consonant "b" on it, the phrase would become "Barry's bizard beaps." In the next example, the initial /p/ could be changed to an /s/ or a /t/. "Peter Piper picked a peck of pickled peppers" becomes "Seter Siper sicked a seck of sickled seppers" or "Teter Tiper ticked a teck of tickled teppers."

If the student is having difficulty handling the deletion and the substitution, the teacher could attempt this activity with just the deletion. In this version of the game, the teacher reads one of the phrase cards and the student deletes the initial sound. For example, after deleting the initial /p/ sound, "Peter Piper picked a peck of pickled peppers" would become "Eter iper icked a eck of ickled eppers."

Rhyming Word Games

Recognizing and producing rhyming words can sometimes be difficult. Teachers may need to begin by giving explicit instructions on how to recognize a rhyme. Explain that rhyming words have the same ending sound but different beginning sounds. Providing examples with visual cues is a great way to reinforce this idea. For example, show a picture of a rose or an actual rose, and point to your nose. Explain that "rose" and "nose" start with different sounds, /r/ and /n/ but end with the same sound. Show a picture as you say the words "hand," "toes," and "foot" and ask the students to name the word that ends with the sounds they hear at the end of nose and rose. Continue practicing by playing with other rhyming words.

Another possible activity for producing rhyming words can be done using the traditional children's song "Down by the Bay" (Raffi, 1976). Begin by modeling the first rhyming pair, and then allow students to create their own rhyming pair to be used in the song, or you can provide the first part of the rhyming pair and have students complete the second half.

The song begins with the reoccurring verse:

Down by the bay,
Where the watermelons grow,
Back to my home,
I dare not go,
For if I do,
My mother will say . . .

This verse then follows with a variation on "Did you ever see a _____,
_____ing a _____, down by the bay?" For example, "Did you ever see
a bear, combing his hair, down by the bay?"

The original verse then continues with a new variation of the aforementioned question. Some examples for completion of the question follow:

Did you ever see a cat, wearing a hat?
Did you ever see a bee with a sunburned knee?
Did you ever see a mouse, building a house?
Did you ever see a llama, wearing pajamas?

Syllable Say Game

Explain to students that a syllable is a part of a word, and that words can have
more than one syllable. The number of syllables that you hear when you pronounce a word is the same as the number of vowel sounds in the word. Say
the word "hat." Ask students to repeat the word "hat." Explain that "hat" is
a one-syllable word with one vowel sound. Ask students to place their hand
under their chin and repeat the word "hat." Tell them to feel how their chin
drops when they say the word hat. Say the word "rabbit," and have students
repeat the word. Ask them to hold up one or two fingers to indicate how many
syllables they hear. Then, ask them to put their hand under their chins, say the
word "rabbit" again, and count how many times their chin drops. Say, "The
word rabbit has two syllables and two vowel sounds." Ask, "How many syllables does the word 'rabbit' have?" Students should respond, "Two." Ask,
"How many vowel sounds does the word 'rabbit' have?" Students should
respond, "Two." Repeat this procedure with various multisyllabic words
until students are familiar with the concept. An example of words you might
use are teacher, butterfly, apple, cartoon, elephant, caterpillar, bumblebee,
dinosaur, doctor, window, garden, grasshopper, telephone, octopus, jacket,
hamburger, spaghetti, and umbrella.

As an extension, say the syllable parts of words and have students blend the
parts together to form the words. For example, using the word "strawberry,"
say the syllable: "straw" and have students repeat; say the syllable, "ber," and
have students repeat; and say the syllable, "ry," and have students repeat. Ask
students, "What is the word?" Prompt students to reply, "Strawberry." Repeat
this procedure for practice in blending syllables in spoken words.

The Long and the Short of It Game

Provide each student with two response cards. On one response card, write the vowel approximately two inches tall so it looks long. On the other response card, write the same vowel approximately one inch tall so that it looks short.

Remind students of the different sounds the vowel can make and explain that today they will be using the cards to indicate if the vowel sound in the words they hear represents a long sound or a short sound. Say a word, and ask students to indicate if the sound is long or short by holding up the correct response card.

Phoneme Match

Place cards with the numbers 1, 2, 3, 4, 5, and 6 face up in the center of the table and a set of picture cards in a stack face down on the table. The game can be played by small pairs or small groups of students. The first student turns over the top picture card. The student tells everyone the name of the picture and how many phonemes are in the word. Then the student places the picture card on top of the card representing the correct number of phonemes in the word. Students earn one point for each card placed on the correct number. The student who earns the most points wins.

Phoneme Race

You will need a game board with ten to twenty blank spaces on it, game playing pieces, and a set of cards with pictures. Each student chooses his own unique playing piece. The first student takes the picture card on the top of the pile. He says the name of the picture. He moves one space on the board for each phoneme in the name of that picture. The next child picks the next card and moves one space for each phoneme in that word. The first student to reach the end of the board is the winner. If students are playing independently, you might want to write the correct answer on the back of the cards so they can check their answers.

Sound Chain

This activity works well with content area vocabulary and can be done with small groups of students or an entire class. The teacher begins by saying one word. The next student then must provide a word that begins with the phoneme with which the original word ended. The activity continues around the group until each student has added a word to the chain. For example, in a science unit about plants, the teacher could begin the activity with the word "plants." The next student could give the word "stem." The next student might give the word "moss." The next student could provide the word "seed-ling." The chain could contain as many words as the teacher chooses.

Word Tiles

Give each student a set of alphabet tiles. Tell the students to use their tiles to make the following word: cat. They take the "c," "a," and "t" tiles and arrange them on their desks. Then the teacher dictates a word that would involve a one- or two-letter change to the word, and the students switch their tiles to make the new word. Following is an example of a possible word chain:

Cat-bat-hat-ham-him-hit-hid-did-din-spin

Thumbs Up Thumbs Down

This game can be played anywhere because it requires no special preparation or pieces and it can be used with any phonemic skill such as initial sounds, final sounds, prefixes, suffixes, or medial syllables. The leader says two words. The students put their thumbs up if the identified sound is the same. They put their thumbs down if the sound is different.

REFERENCES

Alic, M. (2006). Auditory Discrimination Test. *Gale Encyclopedia of Children's Health: Infancy through Adolescence*. Retrieved from Encyclopedia.com: http://www.encyclopedia.com/doc/1G2-3447200073.html.

Antunez, B. (2002). English language learners and the five essential components of reading instruction. *Reading Rockets*. Retrieved from https://readingrockets.org/article/english-language-learners-and-five-essential-components-reading-instruction.

Barzilay, P. (2001). Why readers have problems: Vowel pronunciation and syllable types and how they relate to reading. *English Teachers Network*. Retrieved from http://www.etni.org/etnirag/issue1/peggy_barzilay.htm.

Clear English. (n.d.). Stops and continuants. Retrieved from http://www.paulnoll. com/Books/Clear-Speech/Clear-p12-stops-T-Th.html.

Common Core State Standards Initiative. (2014). English Language Arts Standards Reading: Foundational Skills: Kindergarten. Retrieved from www.corestandards. org/ELA-Literacy/RR/K.

Dechant, E. (1993). *Whole Language Reading*. Lancaster, PA: Techonic.

English Plus. (2014). *Schwa*. Retrieved from http://englishplus.com/grammar/0000 0383.htm.

Hagan, E. C. (2010). Response to intervention: Implications for Spanish-speaking English language learners. *RTI Action Network*. Retrieved from http://www.rtin etwork.org/learn/diversity/response-to-intervention-implications-for-spanish-spe aking-english-language-learners.

Hudson, R. (2005). Word work strategies to develop decoding skills for beginning readers. *Reading First Summer Institute*. Retrieved from http://www.fcrr.org/staff presentations/rhudson/word_work_rf_longisland_fcrr.pdf.

Lane, H. B. (2007). *Phonological Awareness: A Sound Beginning*. Retrieved from http://curry.virginia.edu/reading-projects/projects/garf/Lane-GA_RF_PA_Hand outpdf.pdf.

Lyon, G. R. (1995). Toward a definition of dyslexia. *Annals of Dyslexia, 45*, 3–27.

Moats, L. (2003). *Teacher Knowledge Survey*. Retrieved from http://www.umich.edu /~rdytolrn/pathwaysconference/presentations/moats.pdf.

Moats, L. (2009). Knowledge foundations for teaching reading and spelling. *Read Write, 22*, 379–399. Retrieved from http://www.academia.edu/2063098/Knowledg e_foundations_for_teaching_reading_and_spelling.

Moats, L., & Tolman, C. (2009). Phonological instruction for older students. *Reading Rockets*. Retrieved from https://readingrockets.org/article/phonological-instruc tion-older-students.

Reading Rockets. (n.d.). *Phonological and Phonemic Awareness*. Retrieved from http://www.readingrockets.org/helping/target/phonologicalphonemic.

Silverstein, S. (2005). *Runny Babbit*. New York: HarperCollins.

Sousa, D. (2005). *How the Brain Learns to Read*. Thousand Oaks, CA: Corwin.

Stanovich, K., ed. (1994). Romance and reality [Distinguished Educator Series]. *The Reading Teacher, 47*(4), 280–291.

Straugler, K. (2007). Literacy rubric. Retrieved from http://www.louisianabelieves.c om/docs/default-source/academic-standards/kathy-staugler-literacy-rubric-07.pdf? sfvrsn=2.

University of Oregon. (n.d.). Big ideas in beginning reading: Phonemic awareness. Retrieved from http://reading.uoregon.edu/big_ideas/pa/pa_sequence.php.

Chapter 4

Decoding, Phonics, and Word Analysis

LITERARY CONNECTION

The old man showed an early knack for consonants. Sometimes he got m and n mixed up, but the only one that gave him trouble day in and day out was c. It reminded him of a bronc some cowboy dared him to ride in his Texas League days. He would saddle up the c, climb aboard and grip the pommel for dear life, and ol' c, more often than not, it would throw him. Whenever that happened, he'd just climb right back on and ride 'er some more. Pretty soon c saw who was boss and gave up the fight. But even at their orneriest, consonants were fun. Vowels were something else. He didn't like them and they didn't like him. (Spinelli, 1990, p. 101)

CLASSROOM SCENARIO

After reviewing her reading data from her class' midyear benchmark assessment, Mrs. Smith felt concerned. Her struggling readers were not showing much progress. She had elicited the help of a volunteer to practice the sight vocabulary words with her students. She had provided time for independent reading in class, modeled fluent reading, and used a plethora of comprehension strategies, but her struggling readers were simply not making progress. She actually hadn't needed the benchmark assessment to tell her that; she could hear it when they read aloud in small groups.

Mrs. Smith observed Thomas carefully as he read the book about dinosaurs that he had selected for his independent reading.

"A dinosaur with p-l-a-t-s and s-p-i-k-s is called a stegosaurus. The stegosaurus is a h-e-b-b-or or p-l-a-nt eater. A full gr-ou-n stegosaurus is 30 feet long and 14 feet tall and can w-w- I don't know that word."

"'Eigh' often says /ā/," Mrs. Smith interjected. "What does this letter say?" She pointed to the "w."

"Wuh," Thomas responded.

"Put those two sounds together. Wuh plus /ā/," Mrs. Smith encouraged.

"/Wuh/ /ā/," Thomas said looking puzzled. He still had no idea what the word was.

"Listen as I say the word, Thomas, and tell me what you hear." Mrs. Smith pointed to the "w" and said /wuh/, then immediately pointed to the "eigh" and said /ā/. She ran her finger under the word and said quickly, "/wā/. Can you say this word now?" she asked.

Thomas read the word "weigh."

"Let's look at the sentence." Mrs. Smith read, "A full-grown stegosaurus is 30 feet long and 14 feet tall and can weigh as much as 5 tons, but it has a brain about the size of a dog."

"What an interesting book you have, Thomas. Do you remember what I said e-i-g-h often says?"

Thomas nodded and said, "/ā/."

"That is correct. What is this word?" Mrs. Smith wrote the word "eight" on the whiteboard.

"Eight!" Thomas quickly responded.

"That's right!" Mrs. Smith smiled. "Put a "w" in front of it and what is your new word?"

"Wuh - āt," he said.

"So we just looked at three words with 'eigh': weigh, weight, and eight! Good work today, but time is up so take your book with you back to your seat."

Thomas took his book and sat down at his desk. Mrs. Smith thought about the words with which he had struggled: two CVCe words, "plates" and "spikes"; the multisyllabic word, "herbivore"; the /ow/ sound in grown; and of course the /eigh/ in weigh. She decided that tomorrow she would give Thomas a quick phonics screener so she could pinpoint the exact phonics skills with which he needed help.

WHAT IS DECODING?

In our first literary connection, Jerry Spinelli's *Maniac Magee*, the protagonist undertakes the task of teaching Grayson, an old man who took Maniac under his wing, how to read. The excerpt illustrates Grayson's struggle with phonics and compares it to riding a "bronc." The ride wasn't always smooth and sometimes he got thrown, but he would always climb right back on and try again. Decoding is not a skill that all of our students master with ease, but mastery of the skill will assist students with automaticity, which is fast and accurate word recognition.

Decoding moves the student from phonemic awareness, or the ability to identify, delete, add, and blend sounds, to understanding the relationship between the sound and the symbol. Some of our written symbols, or graphemes, are distinct and cause little difficulty for the beginning reader. Others are very similar in appearance and tend to cause confusion. As beginning readers are developing an understanding of the symbols, confusion sometimes exists because of the similarity between "b" and "d," "b" and "p," "m" and "n," and "q" and "p" (Hudson, 2005).

Decoding is a broad category that includes various strategies students use to determine the pronunciation of unknown words. It is the ability to apply an understanding of the sound–symbol relationship so students can correctly pronounce the written words. These skills enable a student to quickly recognize familiar words and to determine unfamiliar words (Reading Rockets, n.d.).

Ehri (1998) indicated that children progress through phases in their word recognition ability. They begin at the pre-alphabetic phase, and continue moving through the partial alphabetic phase, the full alphabetic phase, the consolidated alphabetic phase, and finally the automatic phase. The goal of decoding instruction is to enable students to easily and rapidly identify words based on successful alphabetic and decoding skills (Ehri, 1998). Decoding provides students with multiple ways to learn about words and their meaning, spelling, and sound. Teaching sound symbol relationships is important, but the role these skills play in expanding vocabulary and building meaning is also important (Juel, Biancaroasa, Coker, & Deffes, 2003). The decoding process involves more than just phonics. Decoding involves building a sight vocabulary, learning to apply structural analysis skills, and developing effective phonics skills at the phoneme, syllable, and morpheme levels.

LITERARY CONNECTION

Little Jack Horner
Sat in the corner,
Eating a Christmas pie;
He put in his thumb,
And pulled out a plum,
And said "What a good boy am I!"
(Author unknown)

USING LITERATURE TO TEACH PHONICS

As brief as the nursery rhyme "Little Jack Horner," our second literacy connection, is, it can be used to teach a variety of phonics lessons. One possible
activity is that teachers could focus on short vowel sounds by highlighting the
single-syllable words with short vowels: *sat, in, jack, put, thumb, plum, and,
am.* Poetry can also lend itself to teaching word patterns such as in the words
Horner and *corner,* which illustrate the r-controlled vowel pattern. The poem
could be used as a scavenger hunt to find words with the silent letters, or you
could have students find all of the two-syllable words and break the words
into syllables. Word patterns form the backbone of phonics instruction and
are often found in poetry.

WHAT IS PHONICS?

Phonics encompasses the practices that "emphasize how spellings are related
to speech sounds in systemic ways that can be used to help the reader decode
unknown words" (Ruetzel & Cooter, 2011, p. 160). The role of phonics in
reading instruction has been debated as far back as the Great Debate (Chall,
1967) when there were two distinct schools of thought about whether or not
to teach phonics. However, the debate is no longer between whether to teach
phonics or not to teach phonics but the when, where, and how of teaching
phonics.

Research supports the following principles for effectively teaching initial
phonics skills.

- Letter-sound relationships need to be taught explicitly and in isolation. However, there is no set rate for presenting new letter-sound correspondences. The appropriate rate differs from child to child.
- The order of presentation should be planned to permit students to quickly read printed texts and materials being used within the classroom.
- More frequently used letter-sound pairs should be presented before less frequently used letter-sound pairs.
- Teachers should begin by teaching consonant letter-sound pairs that can be pronounced in isolation without distortion such as the letters f, m, s, and r.
- To avoid confusion, instruction of letters with similar sounds should not be presented in proximity. For example, the short a and the short e make very similar sounds. Make sure that the child has mastered one before the other is introduced.
- Once single-letter and sound combinations are mastered, consonant blends such as br and gl, consonant clusters such as spl and spr, and consonant digraphs such as ch and th should be taught (Test Prep Books, 2018).

Phonics instruction is an important component of a comprehensive reading program and is just one type of word analysis skill that students need to be able to use in decoding unknown words (National Institute of Child Health and Human Development, 2000). Other decoding skills would include structural analysis and the teaching of sight words. Structural analysis involves combining the smaller letter–sound patterns of phonics into the larger chunks of prefixes, roots or bases, and suffixes. These larger groupings of affixes help to develop children's ability to infer meaning while expanding their vocabulary knowledge. For example, if a student knows that the prefix *bi* means two, twice, or once in every two, they will have a clue when determining the meaning of words containing *bi* such as bicycle, binocular, biped, bilingual, bimonthly, or biweekly.

TYPES OF PHONICS INSTRUCTION

An ongoing phonics debate focuses on what method to use in phonics instruction. Advocates of whole language indicate that phonics should be taught in context as the need arises. Opponents of this method indicate that naturally occurring phonics is not systematic enough. There is also a third, more middle of the road position that combines naturally occurring phonics with explicit instruction. Stahl, Duffy-Hester, and Stahl (1998) conducted research on phonics instruction. Their findings indicated that there are several effective types of phonics instruction, but they were not able to find any support for one method of phonics instruction being superior to any other. The National Reading Panel (2000), based on its review of methods for teaching phonics, found that phonics instruction should be explicit and systematic. They also found that there was not a significant difference between the "effectiveness" of different types of explicit phonics instruction.

There are four basic methods for phonics instruction. Synthetic, analytical, analogy, and embedded phonics instruction are all recognized methods. Synthetic phonics instruction begins by teaching the sounds of the letters. After the letter sounds are mastered, students learn to form words by blending those individual sounds together. Analytic phonics instruction requires students to analyze the common phonemes within the word. Students might examine how the following words are alike: camp, pat, pint, pat, splat, and drop. From this activity, students would determine for themselves that the "p" grapheme says /p/. Analogy phonics instruction begins with exposing the students to a rime. The rime would be the vowel and all of the consonants following it in a single-syllable word such as the –at in the word cat. The students analyze the rime to learn about word families, or other words ending with the same rimes. Embedded phonics is more of a whole-language approach. Embedded phonics is not systematic. In this type of phonics instruction, while students are reading, the teacher may notice that students need help with decoding a particular word as Ms. Smith did with Thomas. The teacher will take that opportunity to stop and instruct the students how to decode that specific word within the context of the lesson.

PHONICS KNOWLEDGE

Since we are all proficient readers, it would seem that we should possess all of the phonics information we need to be effective teachers. Interestingly, Cunningham et al. (2004) noted that not all teachers possess the technical knowledge to teach phonics effectively. They also found that phonics instruction for older struggling readers required "a deeper knowledge and confidence in working with the inconsistencies in English orthography" (p. 510). Consequently, a knowledgeable teacher is essential for effectively scaffolding students' phonics instruction, especially the phonics instruction that needs to be provided for older struggling readers.

Teacher Knowledge Survey

We looked at the "Teacher Knowledge Survey" questions on phonological awareness in the previous chapter. Moats also examined decoding knowledge in her survey of primary teachers. See how your knowledge compares to that of the primary teachers in her sample. The percentage after each of the five questions indicates the percentage of primary teachers in her sample who answered each question correctly.

1. Which of the following has a prefix? Pick one. (9 percent)
   missile, distance, commit, interest, furnish
2. Which of the following has an adjective suffix? Pick one. (7 percent)
   natural, apartment, city, encircle, emptiness
3. The /k/ sound in lake and lack are spelled differently. Why is lack spelled with a ck? (52 percent)
   A. The /k/ sound ends the word.
   B. The word is a verb.
   C. The combination ck is used immediately after a short vowel.
   D. The letters c and k produce the same sound.
   E. There is no principle or rule to explain this.
4. Why is there a double n in stunning? (50 percent)
   A. Because the word ends in a single consonant preceded by a single vowel, and the ending begins with a vowel.
   B. Because the final consonant is always doubled when adding –ing.
   C. Because the letter u has many different pronunciations.
   D. Because the consonant n is not well articulated and needs to be strengthened.
   E. There is no principle or rule to explain this.
5. Which of the following is a feature of English spelling? (10 percent)
   A. A silent e at the end of the word always makes the vowel long.
   B. Words never end in the letters "j" and "v."
   C. When two vowels go walking, the first one does the talking.

D. A closed syllable must begin with a consonant.

E. All of the above.

Answers

You can review the correct answers and the explanations for those answers in the following section. The correct answer to each question is in italics.

1. Which of the following has a prefix? Pick one. (9 percent)
   missile, distance, *commit*, interest, furnish
2. Which of the following has an adjective suffix? Pick one. (7 percent)
   natural, apartment, city, encircle, emptiness
3. The /k/ sound in lake and lack are spelled differently. Why is lack spelled with a ck? (52 percent)
   A. The /k/ sound ends the word.
   B. The word is a verb.
   C. *The combination ck is used immediately after a short vowel.*
   D. The letters c and k produce the same sound.
   E. There is no principle or rule to explain this.
4. Why is there a double n in stunning? (50 percent)
   A. *Because the word ends in a single consonant preceded by a single vowel, and the ending begins with a vowel.*
   B. Because the final consonant is always doubled when adding –ing.
   C. Because the letter u has many different pronunciations.
   D. Because the consonant n is not well articulated and needs to be strengthened.
   E. There is no principle or rule to explain this.
5. Which of the following is a feature of English spelling? (10 percent)
   A. A silent e at the end of the word always makes the vowel long.
   B. *Words never end in the letters "j" and "v."*
   C. When two vowels go walking, the first one does the talking.
   D. A closed syllable must begin with a consonant.
   E. All of the above.

The first question attempts to gauge the teacher's understanding of the role of affixes in structural analysis. Affixes are any group of letters that can be added to a root or base word that changes its meaning, tense, number, or part of speech in some way. In the first question, "commit" is the only word with a prefix. Even though mis, dis, and in are common English prefixes, they would not be considered prefixes in the answer choices provided because they are not used before a root or base word. A prefix is a unit of letters with a specific meaning. The group of letters is placed in front of a root or base word and is used to change or modify the meaning of the word. For a word to have a prefix, you need to be able to remove the prefix and still have a root or base word. A root word is a portion of a word that is generally derived from Greek or Latin. In the case of the word "commit," "com" is the prefix that means "with" or "together." The root word is "mit," which means to send. Although the other choices might appear to have prefixes, when you attempt to separate the prefix from the root word, you are not left with a root or base word.

Base words would be those words that can be used by themselves as a recognizable word in the English language. For example, the word "rejecting" has the suffix "ing," which indicates its tense. "Reject" is the base word. The root word of "rejecting" is "ject" from Latin and means "throw."

The second question also focuses on structural analysis and asks about suffixes. A suffix can modify or change the meaning of a word as well as indicate the number or part of speech: noun, verb, adjective, or adverb. For example, some suffixes change the function of the word by changing a verb into a noun, like -ment does when added to the word govern to form government. Suffixes can also be used to show tense, number, and comparisons. Consequently, affixes, both prefixes and suffixes, can help students understand the meaning of the word (Sophia Learning, 2014). "Natural" is the only word in the list that takes a noun, nature, and changes it to an adjective, natural, through the use of the "al" suffix. "Emptiness" takes the verb empty and makes it a noun by adding the suffix "ness." "Apartment," "city," and "encircle" do not have suffixes. An understanding of structural analysis helps students expand their vocabulary and determine the meaning of unknown words.

Questions 3–5 attempt to gauge the teacher's understanding of the rules that govern the encoding, or spelling, of the sound–symbol relationships. In question 3, the encoding of the letters is not determined by the part of speech or the phonemes. In English, the "ck" combination is used immediately following a short vowel. We do not use "ck" when the vowel sound is long. When there is a long vowel sound, we simply write the letter "k," such as in the word "bike."

In the fourth question, the final consonant is doubled when adding a suffix beginning with a vowel when the root word ends with a single consonant after a short vowel. The word "stun" becomes "stunning" because there is one vowel, a "u," followed by one consonant, an "n," before a suffix beginning with a vowel. This rule explains the encoding differences between the word "hoping" and "hopping." When the vowel was short in the word "hop," we needed to double the final consonant before adding the suffix. The rule says when there is one vowel followed by one consonant, double the consonant before adding a suffix beginning with a vowel. However, if we were changing "boat" to "boating," we do not need to double the final "t" because there are two vowels in the base word.

As you look at the final question, you will note that only 10 percent of the sample of primary teachers was able to answer the question correctly! Obviously, this was a particularly difficult question. The first answer choice is incorrect because a final silent "e" does not always make the vowel long, as demonstrated in the word "have." The third choice, although a cute rhyme, is actually true only about 40 percent of the time (Learning Press, 2014). For example, in the word "thief," even though it has two vowels together, the second one is making the long vowel sound. The fourth answer choice indicates that a closed syllable begins with a consonant. The essential feature of a closed syllable is that the syllable must contain one vowel that makes a short sound and the syllable ends in a consonant. Often closed syllables begin with a consonant; however, closed syllables can begin with a vowel. The first syllable in the word "Indian," "in," is an example. In the word "Indian," the closed syllable begins with a vowel but it still follows the pattern for a closed syllable. The only answer choice that is left is that in English, words do not end with "j" or "v." This actually explains why the word "have" ends in an "e" rather than a "v."

Teachers need an extensive understanding of English phonology and morphology so that they can help students master the decoding and encoding processes. Cunningham and Cunningham (2002) found that research supported teaching children orthographic and morphological patterns and analogy decoding. Hiebert (1999) stressed the importance of students having the opportunity to use multiple types of texts on a regular basis so that students develop proficiency in using sight-word-oriented, decoding-oriented, and meaning-oriented cues in reading. Teachers need to be proficient using all of these approaches to help students to develop skills in the decoding strand.

WHERE SHOULD PHONICS INSTRUCTION BEGIN?

Grapheme–Phoneme Relationships

Phonics instruction begins with developing the basic understanding that graphemes are used to represent phonemes. After students have mastered the individual phoneme, they progress to learning about phonograms. Phonograms are a series of letters that are used to represent a larger sound. This sound could be part of a syllable, a syllable, or other combinations such as an onset and rime, body and coda. A syllable is a unit of pronunciation having only one vowel sound, with or without surrounding consonants. A syllable can form the whole word or be only a part of a word. The body is the part of the syllable through the vowel, and the coda is the portion of the syllable following the vowel. For example, in the word "strand," the body is "stra" and the coda is the "nd."

Word families are groups of words that have common features or patterns. The "–at" word family would be one example. This combination of letters can be found at the end of at least eighteen different English words. Although often referred to as word families, they are also called rimes. A rime is the part of a one-syllable word that begins at the vowel and extends to the end of the word. Instruction in rimes or word families is very appropriate for helping beginning readers quickly expand their sight vocabulary. Teachers need to provide frequent opportunities for students to use manipulative letters or to write to help reinforce these developing skills.

In English because consonant sounds are more obvious than vowel sounds, students typically recognize consonant sounds before vowel sounds. C, g, and y are probably the most difficult of the consonants because they can make multiple sounds. Teachers should know that the letter c will make an /s/ or soft sound when it is followed by the vowels e, i, and y, such as in "cell," "city," and "cycle." In most other instances, it will make a /k/ or hard sound such as in "cup" and "tack" (Carver & Pantoja, 2009). The letter g follows the same pattern. It will make a /j/ or soft sound when it is followed by e, i, or y such as in "gem," "giant," and "gym"; otherwise, it will make a /g/ or hard sound such as in "garden" and "bag." The letter y sometimes acts as a vowel, and sometimes it is a consonant. It acts as a consonant in the word "yes." However, it can also make three different vowel sounds, long /ī/, short /ĭ/, or long /ē/ sound. At the end of a single or first syllable, it will make the long

/ī/ sound like in the words "by" or "plywood." At the end of a multisyllabic word, it tends to make the long /ē/ sound like in "baby," and when the y is in the middle of the syllable it tends to make a short /ĭ/ sound as in the "gym" (Carver & Pantoja, 2009).

Consonant digraphs are two consonants that are used together to form one speech sound or phoneme; for example, ch, ph, and ng each has one distinct sound. The sh digraph makes one sound but can be encoded in a variety of ways—sh, ci, ti, or si—depending on the actual word. The th digraph actually can make two different sounds; the voiceless sound as in "bath" or the voiced sound as in "than."

Initial and final consonant blends or clusters occur when two or more consonants are used together but where each of the phonemes within the blend can be distinguished. However, when two identical consonants are used together in a word, they typically make only one sound as in the word "attic."

Brazilay (2001) observed that vowel patterns can be particularly difficult for beginning readers. She recommended, when teaching vowel sounds, to begin with those vowel patterns that have only one sound and are relatively regular. Regular vowel sounds with consistent spelling, about 75 percent of the time or more, would include ay as /ā/, oa as /ō/, ee as /ē/, ai as /ā/, ey as /ē/, aw as /aw/, oy as /oi/, oi as /oi/, and au as /aw/. These vowel digraphs occur when two vowels are used with a single syllable to produce one vowel sound.

Vowel Combinations Making Multiple Sounds

Once students have mastered the more regular sound–symbol relationships, vowel combinations that make two different sounds should be introduced. Many of these are vowel diphthongs. Diphthongs occur when two vowels are used together to produce a single sound that is neither long nor short but is a third totally different sound such as the /oi/ in oil. These would include ow as /ō/ and /au/, ew as /oo/ and /ū/, oo as /oo/ and /ŭ/, ei as /ā/ and /ē/, ie as /ē/ and /ī/, and ea as /ē/ and /ĕ/. These sounds are more difficult, and students will need practice before they are confident decoding them.

Finally, the two-vowel combination with three possible pronunciations should be taught. These would include ou as /au/, /ŭ/, and /ou/ and oe as /ō/,

/oo/, and /ŭ/. Brazilay (2001) further observed that knowledge of syllable types and vowel combinations, although they do not provide all the answers, will help students better determine which vowel pronunciation to use when they encounter an unknown word. Fluent reading depends on the student's ability to analyze and recognize multisyllabic words. Although multisyllabic words do not occur as frequently as sight words, the ability to decode them easily is important because they tend to carry a significant amount of the meaning and content of a passage (Cunningham, 1998).

The schwa sound can be particularly difficult for students because it occurs in an unaccented syllable and is pronounced as /uh/. It is the most common vowel sound in English, but it is only found in words with two or more syllables (Nordquist, 2014). Encoding this sound is particularly difficult since any of the vowels can be used to represent this sound, such as the second syllables in "women" or "politics."

Morphemes

Ehri (2002) also indicated that understanding simple grapheme–phoneme relationships is not enough. Proficient readers need to develop more advanced phonics skills. She stated that students need to be able to identify word patterns or chunks because this is helpful in decoding multisyllabic words. Those word chunks might be both morphemes, the smallest unit of meaning in English, and syllables.

English words are composed of two different types of morphemes, free and bound. Free morphemes can be used alone as a base or root word like "tie." Bound morphemes can only be used in conjunction with other morphemes, such as the prefix "un." We can combine the free morpheme "tie" with the bound morpheme "un" to create the new word "untie." Familiarity with morphemes can aid in decoding, spelling, and making sense of unknown words.

Syllabic Instruction

These chunks that Ehri (2002) referred to could also include syllables. In order to decode multisyllabic words, students need to know that each syllable contains a single vowel sound, how to divide words into syllables, and how to recombine these syllables into a word. Additionally, students need to be able to recognize the six syllable types, and they must understand their impact on pronunciation. The syllable type is determined by the way the vowels (V) and consonants (C) are arranged within the syllable. This knowledge and understanding of the function of syllables distinguishes phonics instruction for older struggling readers from the single phoneme-grapheme phonics instruction provided in the primary grades.

Because short vowel sounds are generally more consistent, instruction should begin with exposure to closed (CVC) syllables. A closed syllable is one where a single short vowel sound is followed by a consonant as in the words "cat" and "in." Moats (2009) found that closed syllables are one of the most common spelling units and make up almost 50 percent of the syllables with texts.

The other five types of syllables are CV, R Control, CVVC, CVCe, and Cle. Open (CV) syllables would be those that end with a single long vowel sound, such as in "he," "pea," or each of the syllables in the word "veto." R-controlled syllables would be those in which the vowel is followed by a single letter "r"; consequently, the vowel does not make either a long or short sound. Instead, it makes a third sound, such as in the words "chart" or "target." The fourth type of syllable would be the vowel team (CVVC) syllable. These syllables contain two letters that form one vowel sound, and the syllable ends in a consonant. These vowel combinations could make a long sound as in "bead," a short sound as in "bread," or a diphthong sound as in "boil." The silent "e" (CVCe) type of syllable has a long vowel sound followed by a silent "e" pattern, such as in the words "tape" and "stride" and is typically found at the end of the word such as the second syllable in the word "combine." The final syllable type is the Consonant le (Cle). This unaccented syllable is found at the end of a multisyllabic word, such as "apple" or "table" (Hudson, 2005).

No matter how phonics is taught, research indicates it certainly needs to be taught whether to beginning readers, to struggling older readers, or to English language learners. Students must have strategies for decoding words they do not recognize in a text. If a word does not sound right or make sense, students need strategies to determine the word that would make sense in the sentence. Often students have words in their listening and speaking vocabularies that are not in their reading vocabulary. One goal of decoding is to move these words into students' reading vocabulary. Well-developed phonics skills are integral to students' comprehension.

ASSESSMENTS

Phonics assessments and phonics programs are plentiful. The phonics assessment in this chapter is an example of how a teacher can determine a student's phonics strengths and weaknesses using a grade-level text.

This particular assessment would be administered in a one-to-one setting. Two copies of the passage are necessary. The student is given the unmarked passage, and the teacher uses the passage with the italicized words. The teacher circles mispronounced words on the italicized copy as the student reads the passage aloud. The teacher may decide to circle all mispronunciations, but the italicized words are the ones being targeted for this assessment. When giving a phonics assessment of this type, the teacher would choose a passage that reflects the phonics patterns that are being addressed in class.

After marking the words, the teacher will transfer the data to the assessment matrix (see table 4.1). The words are listed on the matrix in the order they appear in the passage. If the student misses the word "this" in the passage, the teacher would circle the X under the CVC column in the row where "this" is listed on the matrix. Another example is if the student says /fā/ correctly in the word "favor," but misses the second syllable /vor/; in this case, the teacher would circle the second X under the "R Control" column but not the first because the student pronounced that syllable correctly.

This procedure is repeated for each missed word. Add the number of circled "X's" in each column and subtract that number from the total at the bottom of the column. This provides the number correct in each category. Divide the number correct by the number of possible responses. This is the percentage of correct responses for each phonetic skill. Using this procedure, the teacher can determine whether mastery has been achieved or identify areas for reteaching (Carver & Pantoja, 2009).

Passage for Phonics Assessment—Student Copy

This morning I woke up startled by the sound of screaming birds outside my window. I wrapped my pillow around my head, but it did not help much. I tumbled out of bed, tripped on my shoes by the side of the night table, and looked at my alarm clock. Woops! It was nine o'clock, and I was really late

Table 4.1   Phonics Assessment Matrix

Word	CVC	CV	Cle	R Control	CVCe	Suffix	Prefix	CVVC	C/G	Sh
this	X									
morning				X		X				
woke					X					
startled			X	X		X				
sound								X		
screaming						X		X		
birds				X		X				
outside					X			X		
my		X								
window	X							X		
wrapped	X					X				
pillow	X	X								
around								X		
help	X									
much	X									
tumbled	X		X			X				
out								X		
tripped	X					X				
side					X					
table		X	X							
alarm		X		X						
woops						X		X		
o'clock	X	X								
really						X		X		
late					X					
school								X		
those					X					
noisy						X		X		
birds				X		X				
favor		X		X						
star				X						
Total	/9	/6	/3	/7	/5	/11	/	/10	/	/

CVC: Consonant–vowel–consonant syllable; CV: Consonant–vowel syllable; Cle: Consonant–le syllable; R-control: R-control syllable; CVCe: Consonant–long vowel–consonant–silent E syllable; CVVC: Consonant–vowel combination–consonant syllable; C/G: Soft or hard C or G phonemes; Sh: The phoneme Sh as encoded in various ways: sh, ci, si, ti.

for school. Those noisy birds did me a favor. I did not want to miss school today. It was the day of the big game and I was the star player.

Passage for Phonics Assessment—Teacher Copy

This morning I *woke* up *startled* by the *sound* of *screaming birds outside my window.* I *wrapped* my *pillow around* my head, but it did not *help* much. I *tumbled out* of bed, *tripped* on my shoes by the *side* of the night table and looked at my *alarm* clock. *Woops!* It was nine *o'clock,* and I was *really late* for *school. Those noisy birds* did me a *favor.* I did not want to miss school today. It was the day of the big game and I was the *star* player.

PHONICS ACTIVITIES

Syllable War

This game is played by two players and is similar to the card game War. However, the major difference is that instead of using a normal deck of cards, you will need a set of at least twenty blank cards. On each blank card, you will need to write one content area word. Make sure to include a combination of single-syllable and multisyllabic words. The deck of cards is divided evenly between the players. Both players turn over their top card at the same time and place it with the word facing up in the center of the table. Each player determines the number of syllables in his word. The player that has the word with the most syllables takes both cards if he can read the words on the cards. If he cannot read both words correctly, the cards remain in the center of the table until the next set of cards is played. The winner of the next set takes all the cards. At the end of the game, or when time is called, the player with the most cards wins the game.

Build a Word

Remind students that when the syllable ends with a vowel, the vowel usually makes the long sound. Vowels in the middle of the syllable tend to make the short vowel sound. In Cle syllables, the /le/ makes the sound in the end of the word "table." When a vowel is followed by an "r," the "r" changes the vowel

Table 4.2   Build a Word

roc	ket	cat	tle	he
ro	ca	ble	bat	tle
con	tact	fin	ish	mi
nus	hu	mid	su	Per
wig	gle	pre	vent	pho
ny	py	thon	Sta	ple

sound so that the sound is neither long nor short, but instead the vowel makes the R-control sound as in the words "chart," "dirt," or "porch."

For this game, you will need the chart (see table 4.2), a blank sheet of paper, and a timer. Students may work individually or in teams. Display the syllable chart from table 4.2 for four minutes. The time limit can be adjusted based upon the needs of your students. The goal of this game is for students to combine two of the syllables to form a real two-syllable word. One point is awarded for each real word the student writes on the paper before time is called.

Winning Vowel Teams

You will need a set of blank cards. There should be enough cards for each student in your class to have one card. On each card, write one of the following vowel teams: ai, ea, ee, oa, ue, or ie. Divide the class into teams of equal number. The team members line up one behind the other at a predetermined distance from the board. Each team gets a dry erase marker and a set of vowel team cards. Give the team captain enough cards so that each person on the team could have one.

Each team captain shuffles their team's cards and places them face down on the table. When the teacher says "Begin," the first person on each team turns over the top card. That person reads the vowel team on the card, runs up to the board, and writes a word containing that vowel team. If the player is having difficulty coming up with a word, teammates may help the player. After the first team member writes the word on the board, the player goes back and tags the hand of the next team member. The second team member turns over the next card, goes to the board, and writes a word containing the next vowel team. The first team to finish with the most correctly spelled words on the board is the winning team. One point is awarded for each word the team spells correctly.

Table 4.3   Suffix Chart

Verb Suffixes	Noun Suffixes	Adjective Suffixes	Adverb Suffixes
-es	-age	-able	-ly
-s	-al	-al	-ward
-ed	-ance	-er	-ways
-ing	-ant	-est	-wide
	-ence	-ful	-wise
	-ent	-ic	
	-ar	-ish	
	-ism	-less	
	-ish	-ous	
	-ment	-some	
	-ness		

Add to a Word

Create a set of blank cards so that there are enough cards for each student to have one card. Write one base word on each card. Divide the group of students into teams of equal number. Choose four suffixes from each of the categories in table 4.3 and write those four suffixes on the board.

Each team is given a set of cards so that each team member has one card. The goal is for the team to add a suffix to each word and earn more points than the other teams. Verb suffixes are worth one point. Adjective suffixes are worth two points. Adverb and noun suffixes are worth three points. The team writes down as many base words with suffixes as they can before time is called. The team that creates the most real words and earns the most points is the winner.

Suffix Race

Suffixes can be added to base words in three different ways: just adding the suffix, taking off the final e, or doubling the final consonant in the base or root word. Review the rules for adding suffixes. If the base word ends in an "e," take off the "e" before adding a suffix that begins with a vowel. If there is one vowel followed by one consonant in the base word, double the consonant before adding a suffix that begins with a vowel. In other cases, simply add the suffix to the base word.

List the following base words on the board: glide, sip, pat, spill, boast, camp, flake, stamp, hope, and rip. When the teacher says "Begin," the team works together to add "ing" to each of the base words. One point is awarded for each correctly spelled word. The team that earns the most points by writing the base words and suffixes correctly before time is called is the winner.

Wrapping Up the C

Remind students that the letter "c" can make two different sounds. It makes an /s/ when it is followed by "i," "e," or "y" and a /k/ at the end of the word or when followed by any letter other than "i," "e," or "y." The teacher needs to choose a short piece of text and distribute a copy to each student. For this activity, students may work in groups or individually.

Each student or group of students will attempt to find words containing the letter "c" and correctly identify the sound that the "c" makes in that word. Students should underline the letter after the "c," and then put a box around the letter "c" if it makes the sound in the word "cat." They will place a circle around the letter "c" if it makes the sound in the word "circle."

Students or groups of students earn one point for each word containing a "c" where the sound was correctly identified if the student can read the entire list of words correctly.

Syllable Memory

Create a deck of about 16–20 blank cards. A 3" × 5" note card cut in half would be large enough. Choose eight to ten two-syllable words from the following list: he-ro, in-spect, pre-pare, hu-man, cat-tle, cy-press, ad-mire, pu-pil, suc-cess, can-cel, fur-nish, ton-sil, en-gage, cir-cus, con-fuse, mo-ment, sup-port, re-spite, vic-tim, and cri-sis. Write the first syllable of the word on one card and the second syllable of the word on a different card until you have used all the words.

Spread the cards out on the table face down so that the players cannot see the syllable on the card. The first player turns over two cards. He tries to combine those two syllables to make a real word. If he can make a real word, he gets to keep the two cards and go again. His turn continues until he turns over two cards that cannot be combined to form a real word. He then turns those two cards back over and places them back on the table in the position he took them from. It is then the next person's turn. Play continues until none

Table 4.4   Sh Combinations

glacier	magician	partial	palatial
glacial	sufficient	adoration	conviction
contemplation	mutation	preferential	convention
impression	deficiency	delusion	mansion
office	financial	presidential	invasion
revision	sequential	decision	extension

of the remaining syllable cards can be combined to form real words. Syllables can be combined in various ways to form words, so sometimes there might be cards left over. The player with the most cards at the end of the game is the winner.

The difficulty in this game can be increased by using content area vocabulary. For example, you can choose three syllable content area vocabulary words. However, you will want to make sure that the words you choose have the same number of syllables so students know how many cards to turn over. They would turn over one card for each syllable of the word.

Sh Checkers

Create an 8 square by 8 square checkerboard on a sheet of paper or use a checkerboard from a game of checkers. On each square of the board that would typically be black, type or paste one of the /sh/ sound words from table 4.4. The /sh/ sound can be spelled four different ways in English: "sh," "ci," "ti," or "si."

Place thirteen objects in the black squares on the first three rows on each side of the board. You can use checkers, coins, and so on as long as each player has a set of thirteen objects that are the same. This game is played like checkers. The only difference is that in order to be able to make a move, the student must be able to pronounce the word and identify how the /sh/ is spelled in the square where she wants to move. If a student wants to jump her opponent, she needs to be able to read the words in the squares she is jumping and the word in the square in which she wants to land.

When students are able to read the words on the board easily, the game can be made more difficult by requiring the students to use the words in sentences.

Table 4.5 Syllable Types for Divide and Conquer

CVC	CV	R Control	CVCe	CVVC	Cle
in	de	per	cite	aut	ble
un	he	tor	spire	real	gle
sub	ro	jor	pate	teen	tle
as	pea	jar	use	roud	dle
lug	ma	tern	mate	peer	ple
grad	pre	ber	gage	peach	sle
stum	stu	lar	hope	bean	zle
som	mo	plor	ate	bleed	
ment		ber	brite	frail	

Divide and Conquer

There are six types of syllables. As students become more familiar with the vowel sound and appearance of each of these types, they will be more easily able to recognize them in unfamiliar words. The objective of this game is to divide the syllables into the six types. This game can be played individually or with groups of students. Each group or individual gets a set of cards that contain the syllables listed in table 4.5. When the teacher says "Begin," the group or individual separates the syllables into the six different types. The individual or team that classifies and says the syllable correctly is the winner. As a reference, the syllables are correctly arranged by group in table 4.5.

Morphology

Teach students to break words down into morphemes by following these four steps:

Analyze the word for recognizable morphemes, both roots and affixes. Think of a possible meaning based on the word parts. Check the meaning of the word against the context of the word in the text. Check the dictionary to confirm or check with a peer (Prince, 2010).

REFERENCES

All About Learning Press. (2014). When two vowels go walking. Retrieved from http: //www.allaboutlearningpress.com/when-two-vowels-go-walking/.

Barzilay, P. (2001). Why readers have problems: Vowel pronunciation and syllable types and how they relate to reading. *English Teachers Network*. Retrieved from http://www.etni.org/etnirag/issue1/peggy_barzilay.htm.

Carver, L., & Pantoja, L. (2009). *Teaching Syllables Patterns*. Gainesville, FL: Maupin House.

Chall, J. S. (1967). *Learning to Read: The Great Debate*. New York: McGraw-Hill.

Cunningham, P. C. (1998). The multisyllabic word dilemma: Helping students build meaning, spell, and read 'big' words. *Reading and Writing Quarterly: Overcoming Learning Difficulties, 14*(2), 189–210.

Cunningham, P. M., & Cunningham, J. W. (2002). In A. E. Farstrup & S. J. Samuels (Eds.), *What Research Has to Say about Reading Instruction* (3rd ed., pp. 87–109). Retrieved from http://www-tc.pbs.org/teacherline/courses/rdla155/pdfs/c2s3_7whatweknow.pdf.

Cunningham, A. E., Perry, K. E., & Stanovich, P. J. (2004). Disciplinary knowledge of K-3 teachers and their knowledge calibration in the domain of early literacy. *Annals of Dyslexia, 54*, 139–166.

Ehri, L. C. (1998). Grapheme-phoneme knowledge is essential for learning to read words in English. In J. L. Metsala & L. C. Ehri (Eds.), *Word Recognition in Beginning Literacy* (pp. 3–40). Mahwah, NJ: Erlbaum.

Ehri, L. C. (2002). Phases of acquisition in learning to read words and implications for teaching. In R. Stainthorp & P. Tomlinson (Eds.), *Learning and Teaching Reading* [British Journal of Educational Psychology Monograph Series II]. London: British Journal of Educational Psychology.

Hiebert, E. H. (1999). Text matters in learning to read. *The Reading Teacher, 52*, 552–566.

Hudson, R. (2005). Word work strategies to develop decoding skills for beginning readers. *Reading First Summer Institute*. Retrieved from http://www.fcrr.org/staff presentations/rhudson/word_work_rf_longisland_fcrr.pdf.

Juel, C., Biancarosa, G., Coker, D., & Deffes, R. (2003). Walking with Rosie: A cautionary tale of literacy instruction. *Educational Leadership, 60*(7), 12–18.

Lane, H. B. (2007). Phonological awareness: A sound beginning. Paper presented at the Georgia Reading First 2nd Annual Struggling Reader Conference.

Moats, L. C. (2009). *Language Essentials for Teachers of Reading and Spelling: Module 3: Spellography for Teachers: How English Spelling Works* (2nd ed.). Boston: Sopris West Educational Services.

National Institute of Child Health and Human Development. (2000). *Report of the National Reading Panel: Teaching Children to Read* (National Institutes of Health Pub. No. 00-4769). Washington, DC: Government Printing Office.

National Reading Panel. (2006). *Teaching Children to Read: An Evidence-Based Assessment of the Scientific Research Literature on Reading and its Implications for Reading Instruction* (National Institutes of Health Pub. No. 00-4769). Washington, DC: National Institute of Child Health and Human Development. Retrieved from http://www.nichd.nih.gov/publications/pubs/nrp/Pages/smallbook.aspx.

Nordquist, R. (2014). Schwa. *About Education*. Retrieved from http://grammar.about.com/od/rs/g/Schwa-term.htm.

Prince, R. E. C. (2010). Making the words add up: How morphology-viewing words as a combination of parts-can become an instructional tool for building reading skills. *Usable Knowledge Relevant Research for Today's Educators*. Retrieved from gse.harvard.edu/news/uk/10/07/making-words-add.

Reading Rockets. (n.d.). Word decoding and phonics. In *Helping Struggling Readers*. Retrieved from http://www.readingrockets.org/helping/target/phonics.

Reutzel, D. R., & Cooter, R. B. (2011). *Strategies for Reading Assessment and Instruction: Helping Every Child Succeed*. Boston: Pearson.

Sophia Learning. (2014). Common suffixes and their meanings. Retrieved from http://www.sophia.org/tutorials/common-suffixes-and-their-meanings.

Spinelli, J. (1990). *Maniac Magee*. Boston: Little, Brown & Company.

Stahl, S. A., Duffy-Hester, A. M., & Stahl, K. A. (1998). Everything you wanted to know about phonics (but were afraid to ask). *Reading Research Quarterly, 33*, 338–355.

Chapter 5

Fluency

CLASSROOM VISIT

During small-group instruction, Ms. Smith noticed that Rashad's reading was very choppy. He did not group words together in meaningful ways and seemed to race through the punctuation. He read without expression and didn't appear to be interested in the material. Remembering what he read seemed to be difficult. Although he was often able to answer less complex, knowledge-level questions, sometimes his responses for even the "right-there questions" were incorrect.

Ms. Smith decided to administer a running record so she could collect data to better understand Rashad's reading behaviors. A running record can be used to quickly analyze an individual student's oral reading. While the student is reading a passage orally, the teacher is marking whether the words are read correctly or incorrectly. The teacher tallies the number of errors and analyzes the mistakes. Miscues in pronunciation, substitutions, omissions, and self-corrections are all recorded. Fluency in words per minute can also be calculated.

The running record revealed that Rashad lacked fast, accurate, and effort-less word identification, and did not seem to know what to do when he came to a word he did not recognize. The words he substituted, more often than not, did not make sense in the text. This was a good indication that he was not comprehending as he was reading.

When Ms. Smith asked Rashad what the passage was about, he responded, "It's about these guys, Josh Gibson, Hank Aaron, and a farmer. They all liked baseball and played a lot."

Rashad was able to identify the topic baseball, but he clearly missed the main idea of the text and provided incorrect information because there was not a farmer in the passage at all. Given the amount of words he did not know in the text, this was not surprising. The decoding errors impacted his comprehension of the passage.

After looking at the results from the running record, Ms. Smith was also concerned about Rashad's fluency, so she used a fluency rubric to further evaluate his reading of an instructional-level text because she knew he was reading below grade level. Having worked with Rashad, she had a good idea of a passage that would be at about his instructional level. She chose a level of text where she thought he would score above 94 percent in word identification accuracy. On the Elements of Fluency Rubric, she skipped the accuracy category but placed a checkmark where he scored in each of the other categories (see table 5.1).

Using this particular rubric, a score of 12 or more would indicate that a student was making good progress in fluency. Scores below 12 might indicate that the student needs additional instruction in specific areas. Rashad earned a 2 in the categories of grouping, tempo, and cadence, and he earned a 1 in the reading rate category. Adding those scores together, Rashad earned a score of 7 on the rubric. Since he was reading an instructional-level passage, he would also have earned a 3 in the word identification category. This would give him a total of 10 on the rubric indicating that there were some concerns in the area of fluency.

Ms. Smith decided that the first area she would work on would be reading rate. She began thinking about text selections where the speed could be used to help convey the author's mood. She chose an assortment of scary, funny, silly, and sad stories so that they could begin focusing on conveying the mood through the pace at which Rashad read the story. Ms. Smith also decided to focus on the importance of paying attention to the punctuation.

As observed in the small-group scenario in chapter 1, Rashad generally ignored punctuation when he read, and although he did group some words together, it was not always in a meaningful way. He frequently paused or hesitated as he read. Consequently, Ms. Smith described his reading as labored.

Table 5.1 Elements of Fluency Rubric

Category	1	2	3	4
Word Identification	Immediate recognition of less than 85 percent of the words. Frequent decoding errors.	Recognizes 86–90 percent of the words in the passage.	Recognizes 91–95 percent of the words in the passage.	Recognizes 96–100 percent of the words with automaticity.
Grouping	Words read one at a time, and no attempt is made to group them.	Two or three words are grouped together. Grouping is choppy and not necessarily appropriate.	Sentences are divided mid-sentence and/or read as run-ons.	Groups in appropriate phrases, clauses, or sentences.
Tempo	Pauses frequently and repeats words.	Mixture of smooth reading with difficulty in some spots.	Most of the passage is read smoothly with only occasional areas of difficulty.	Reads smoothly with appropriate pauses.
Reading Rate	Reads too quickly or very slowly.	Reads slowly or rushes through punctuation.	Reads most of the passage at an appropriate rate but not all of it.	Reads at a conversational speed throughout.
Cadence	Reading is monotone.	Begins to occasionally use expression in small portions of the text.	Generally uses expression with few exceptions	Reads with expression that fits the tone of the text.

Adapted from Rasinski (2003).

Rashad's inability to decode unknown words also significantly impacted his ability to read fluently.

LITERARY CONNECTION

A panda walks into a café. He orders a sandwich, eats it,
   then draws a gun and fires two shots into the air.
"Why?" asks the confused waiter, as the panda makes toward the exit. The panda
   produces a badly punctuated wildlife manual and tosses it over his shoulder.
"I'm a panda," he says, at the door. "Look it up."
The waiter turns to the relevant entry and, sure enough, finds an explanation.
"*Panda.* Large black and white bear like mammal, native to China.
   Eats, shoots and leaves." (Truss, 2003, back cover)

WHAT IS FLUENCY?

Fluency has many components. Appropriate phrasing is one important component, as is evidenced from Truss's vignette from the back cover of her amusing book. Because of its many components, defining fluency can be tricky. Some definitions include comprehension and some do not. One definition emphasizes accurate, automatic word recognition and components, such as phonemic awareness and letter–sound correspondences that allow students to rapidly and correctly identify words (Pearson Education, 2010). You will notice that comprehension is not specifically addressed in this definition.

A second definition of fluency is an oral reading performance that demonstrates prosody (Kuhn & Stahl, 2003). Kuhn and Stahl (2003) further expand on their definition to include three separate components of prosody in their definition of fluency: (a) stress (some words may receive more emphasis than others), (b) pitch (the rise and fall in sound patterns), and (c) juncture (appropriate text phrasing). This second definition of fluency focuses only on the understanding of surface-level comprehension necessary for appropriate phrasing of the text.

A third definition of fluency is as a component of oral and silent reading. It recognizes that automaticity and prosody have a reciprocal relationship with comprehension, and that as automaticity and prosody increase, so does comprehension. This definition describes fluency as the bridge to comprehension in both oral and silent reading (Kuhn, Schwanenflugel, & Meisenger, 2010).

Defining fluency is important because a teacher's definition of fluency will likely impact how fluency instruction is provided and assessed in the classroom. If a teacher defines fluency as reading for speed and accuracy, you might see students participating in timed readings. These students would not necessarily be reading with expression but would be reading as fast as they could in an attempt to see how many words they can read correctly in one minute.

In a classroom where a teacher defines fluency as reading with prosody, rhythm, stress, and intonation, you might see students taking turns reading aloud in whole or small groups. Allington suggests that word-by-word reading may be a learned response by the struggling reader who, when reading aloud, often experiences frequent interruptions. While the student is reading orally, the teacher may interrupt, directing the student to sound out words, or other students may interject the correct word (Allington, as cited in Farstrup & Samuels, 2006). If this is a regular practice in the classroom, struggling students may begin to anticipate interruptions and become hesitant as they read (Farstrup & Samuels, 2006).

In a classroom where fluency is tied to comprehension, students may be evaluated for rhythm, stress, and intonation as well as speed and accuracy. Discussion or questioning strategies about the text would be a component of this instructional practice in support of comprehension.

No matter what the definition of fluency, we all recognize fluent readers when we hear them. A fluent reader uses expression, quickly recognizes most words, and appears to read effortlessly. In this chapter, we are going to focus on Kuhn, Schwanenflugel, and Meisenger's (2010) definition of fluency which includes comprehension. They define fluency as a combination of "accuracy, automaticity, and oral reading prosody, which, taken together, facilitate the reader's construction of meaning" (p. 240). Fluency is evidenced through efficient word recognition, appropriate expression and intonation, and understandable word groupings. Fluency is an important factor in both oral and silent reading because it helps support comprehension.

Fluency is the ability to read text with appropriate volume, expression, smoothness, phrasing, and stress. Effective use of prosody involves chunking words into appropriate phrases of meaningful units based on the syntactic features of the text. Fluent reading is the bridge to comprehension and is dependent upon the student having well-developed oral language, phonological awareness, and word recognition skills. Although these skills are important, these skills taught in isolation do not necessarily result in fluent reading (NRP, 2000).

WHAT RESEARCH SAYS

Is fluency instruction necessary, or will it just develop when readers are proficient with the other foundational skills? To analyze fluency development, the National Association of Educational Progress conducted research on the fluency levels of a sample of fourth-grade students. Alarmingly, they found that 44 percent were dysfluent even with a grade-level passage that the students read in supportive conditions. In addition, the study found that fluency and reading comprehension were closely related. Those students who had low fluency scores also scored lower than their peers on comprehension assessments (Pinnell et al., 1995). Hops and Fuchs (2005), in their study of first-through fourth-grade students, found a significant correlation between oral reading fluency and passage comprehension as assessed by the Woodcock Reading Mastery Test. Ardoin, Wit, and Suldo (2004) found scores on a maze silent reading task to be positively correlated to reading comprehension scores. A maze assessment requires students to silently read a timed passage in which every fifth to seventh word has been deleted. Three possible choices are provided for each of the deleted words. Students choose the correct response from the choices provided. The aforementioned studies further supported the National Reading Panel (2000) position that fluency instruction is an important component of a research-based reading program.

One of the first researchers who contributed to the understanding of fluency was William MacKeen Cattell (1886), a nineteenth-century psychologist. He discovered that individuals could *read* a word like "lion" faster than they could *name* the picture representing the feline! Cattell explained that reading becomes almost "automatic." Interestingly, he also determined that proficient readers were more automatic in reading than they were in speech (Wolf, n.d.). Based on these studies, it would seem that people have the ability to learn to read so well that they can do it almost without thinking about it.

However, acquiring fluency is a complex, lengthy, developmental process that requires the reader to have mastered all the foundational skills of reading acquisition. It encompasses all the levels from the sublexical letter fluency through word knowledge to the connected-text level of comprehension. The phonological, orthographic, morphological, syntactic, and semantic cueing systems all contribute to fluent reading. Fluency instruction builds on the foundation of phonemic awareness, letter naming, sound–letter associations, sight words, and oral reading of connected text. Developing the fluency subskills makes them readily available so they can be combined with other skills to perform the more complex task of fluent reading (Learning Point Associates, 2004). For example, when students learn to fluently recognize letters, this promotes the more automatic acquisition of letter sounds, which enhances word recognition and leads to improved comprehension. However, just teaching the skills that lead to fluency is not enough. Carreker (2002) noted that for many striving readers, difficulty in reading manifested itself in a lack of fluency—even when students' decoding skills improved. This further supports that fluency is more than quickly recognizing words.

The importance of fluency instruction for comprehension development is also highlighted in *Put Reading First* (Armbruster, Lehr, & Osborn, 2001), where the impact of fluency development on comprehension was second only to that of vocabulary instruction. Teachers should be as explicit in helping students read fluently as they are in teaching them to decode accurately and build vocabulary knowledge. The National Reading Panel (2000) reported that fluency was often overlooked in classroom instruction. Since that report was published, fluency instruction has begun to receive more attention. However, often reading speed has been mistaken for fluency, and the emphasis has been placed on increasing the number of words read per minute while overlooking the other components of fluency (Pikulski & Chard, 2005).

Fluency is complex and essential to comprehension. It is not about learning to read faster; it is about pacing and phrasing that enable the reader to construct meaning from text, which is the ultimate goal of reading. Although we often think of fluency as the oral reading of a text, students need to develop both oral and silent reading fluency.

In the primary grades, more emphasis tends to be placed on oral reading fluency beginning with letter naming, moving to word and phrase reading, and ultimately moving to connected text or words in sentences or paragraphs.

Fuchs et al. (2001) found that, although oral reading fluency can be computed using words presented in isolation rather than connected text, these two measures seem to be based on different constructs. They found that connected text fluency has a stronger relationship to comprehension than word list fluency. While both are important skills, word list fluency measures word recognition. Even if students recognize words quickly, they may not be fluent readers. Fluency involves not just reading accurately and quickly but with expression and chunking words together meaningfully. Which is better supported with connected text reading at the passage level. As students progress into the intermediate levels, greater demands are placed on developing silent reading fluency. Silent reading fluency is important, but it is more difficult to measure because it is not as observable (Denton et al., 2011). Just because students are reading fluently orally, it does not mean that they are reading fluently silently. Similarly, you cannot assume that just because they are fluent readers that they are comprehending the text.

Although fluency is developmental, it is not a stage of development. A reader's fluency can change depending on background knowledge, familiarity with the content, vocabulary knowledge, reading purpose, and the type and complexity of the text. Extensive background knowledge about a topic will enable readers to remember more information from a passage and read it more fluently (Tankersley, 2003).

Fluency is the ability to read a text accurately, smoothly, quickly, and with expression. It involves automatic word recognition or automaticity, and it is the bridge to comprehension or understanding. If a student does not read fluently, the next step is to determine what is interfering with fluent reading. Fluency is a complex developmental process that builds on all of the early reading skills.

ASSESSING FLUENCY

Ms. Smith used four of the categories from a multidimensional fluency rubric when she was evaluating Rashad's reading. Multidimensional fluency scales are one of the best tools for assessing oral reading fluency (Ruetzel & Cooter, 2011).

As was evident in Ms. Smith's evaluation, a minimum of four different categories should be considered: grouping, tempo, reading rate, and cadence.

For a more extensive assessment, the category of word identification could be added. Contextual grade-level passages have been determined to provide the most reliable measures for calculating reading accuracy (Hudson, Lane, & Pullen, 2005).

To assess reading accuracy or word identification, the student reads a one-minute portion of an unfamiliar grade-level passage. As the student reads, the teacher follows along, marking errors, including mispronunciations, substitutions, and deletions. Words that the student self-corrects as he reads are not counted as errors. The number of words read correctly is divided by the total number of words to yield a percentage correct for the accuracy category. This assessment of accuracy provides for a quantitative measure that can be used in addition to more qualitative measures. There are many fluency rubrics available for teacher use in measuring the qualitative aspects of fluency. Table 5.1 presents one example, and Rasinski's (2003) Multidimensional Fluency Rubric is another excellent example; it includes the qualitative features of expression and volume, phrasing, smoothness, and pace.

Oral Reading Fluency

Oral reading rate assessments can generally be used beginning in first grade (Paris, Paris, & Carpenter, 2001). These assessments could include the multidimensional fluency rubric, a running record, or teacher observation.

As another form of assessment, the teacher could use a one-minute oral reading fluency assessment (ORF). When administering the ORF, the teacher needs two copies of an unfamiliar grade-level passage. The teacher gives the student one copy of the passage and keeps the other. The student orally reads the passage for one minute. While the student is reading, the teacher follows along on the second copy marking any errors. These would include mispronunciations, substitutions, and/or deletions. Words that the student self-corrects while reading are not counted as errors. The number of errors is then subtracted from the total number of words read to calculate the final number of words read correctly per minute. If a portion longer than one minute is read, the total number of correct words is then divided by the number of minutes and seconds for which the student read. Although the ORF measures speed and accuracy, it does not account for the qualitative features of fluency—expression, phrasing, smoothness, and pacing. Although speed and pacing may seem similar, speed is a measure how quickly a student reads while pacing involves more rhythm or tempo.

Oral Reading Rate by Grade

Many researchers have suggested different amounts for the average words correct per minute (wcpm) by grade level at which students should be reading. Table 5.2 lists the suggested average words correct per minute (wcpm) by grade level and researcher. As you can see, there is some discrepancy, but these scores will help you determine whether a student's oral reading rate is above, at, or below grade-level expectations. When assessing oral reading rate, it is important to remember that two elements, reading endurance and reading processing or comprehension, are not addressed by the words correct per minute measure (Reutzel & Cooter, 2011).

Table 5.2   Grade Level Words Correct per Minute by Researcher

Grade	Hasbrouck and Tindal	Rasinski	Manzo	Reading A–Z	Fountas and Pinnell
1	0–53	5–60	30–54	50–70	0–100
2	51–89	53–94	66–104	70–100	90–120
3	71–107	79–114	86–124	100–130	100–140
4	94–123	99–118	95–130	130–140	120–160
5	110–139	105–128	108–140	140–160	140–180
6	127–150	115–145	112–145	160–170	160–200
7	128–150	147–167	112–145	160–170	180–220
8	133–151	156–171	112–145	160–170	180–220

Phrasing and expression can be further analyzed using either a checklist or a scale. Although both phrasing and expression provide important information, you do not obtain the same information from both of them. The National Assessment for Educational Progress (NAEP) (2002) developed the following scale to help determine if the student is a fluent or dysfluent (nonfluent) reader (see table 5.3).

Table 5.3 National Assessment for Educational Progress Oral Reading Fluency Scale

Fluent	Level 4	Reads primarily in larger, meaningful phrase groups. Although some regressions, repetitions, and deviations from text may be present, these do not appear to detract from the overall structure of the story. Preservation of the author's syntax is consistent. Some or most of the story is read with expressive interpretation.
	Level 3	Reads primarily in three- or four-word phrase groups. Some small groupings may be present. However, the majority of phrasing seems appropriate and preserves the syntax of the author. Little or no expressive interpretation is present.
Nonfluent	Level 2	Reads primarily in two-word phrases with some three- or four-word groupings. Some word-by-word reading may be present. Word groupings may seem awkward and unrelated to larger context of sentence or passage.
	Level 1	Reads primarily word by word. Occasional two-word or three-word phrases may occur—but these are infrequent and/or they do not preserve meaningful syntax.

National Assessment of Education Progress (NAEP). (2002). *Oral Reading Study*. Washington, DC: U.S. Department of Education National Center for Education Statistics.

Hudson, Lane, and Pullen Checklist

Hudson, Lane, and Pullen (2005) developed a fluency checklist that can be used to identify students' specific areas of need. This information would be particularly beneficial in planning instruction (see table 5.4).

The information from fluency assessments will help you determine appropriate next steps in fluency instruction. Based upon student needs, you might want to provide instruction in reading rate or speed, expression, appropriate volume, smoothness, or phrasing. Depending on your student's level, instruction might begin with letters, words, phrases, or connected texts. Partner readings, repeated readings, teacher read alouds, and shared reading where the teacher reads a text aloud as students follow along, all support reading fluency. In addition, the following activities can be used to help students improve their reading fluency.

Table 5.4   Fluency Checklist

Student used appropriate stress on important words.

Student's voice rose and fell at appropriate points in the text.

Student's inflection reflected the punctuation.

Student used appropriate vocal tones to represent character's mental state.

Student used punctuation to pause appropriately at phrase boundaries.

Student used prepositional phrases to pause appropriately at phrase boundaries.

Student used subject–verb divisions to pause appropriately at phrase boundaries.

Student paused appropriately to phrase boundaries within the sentence.

Hudson, R. F., Lane, H. B., & Pullen, P. C. (2005). Reading fluency assessment and instruction: What, why, and how? *The Reading Teacher, 58*(8), 702–714.

FLUENCY ACTIVITIES

Speed Read

Create thirty-seven blank cards, and choose six target letters. Write a single target letter on each blank card. Five of the letters will be used six times, and one will be used seven times. Place a timer between two students, and provide students with a sheet to record their time in minutes and seconds for multiple tries.

One student chooses the top card from the stack and places it face up on the table. The other student divides the remaining cards into two stacks of eighteen cards each and gives one of the stacks to the other player. Student 1 starts the timer and says, "Begin." Each student turns over one card and quickly says the name of the letter. If the letter matches the target letter, the student places it on top of the target letter. If it does not match, the student places the card to the side. Play continues until students use all of their cards. Student 1 stops the timer and records the time on the time record sheet. The students reverse roles and play again, attempting to increase both speed and accuracy.

Alphabet Match

You will need plastic uppercase letters and a timer. Create a game board by writing the uppercase letters of the alphabet on the board in a circle (approximately the size of a large pizza). Place the plastic uppercase letters in the center of the circle. This activity can be played by individuals or small groups of students. Set the timer for two minutes. The first student selects a plastic letter from the center pile, names it, and places it on the corresponding alphabet letter written on the board. The student repeats this process with as many of the letters as possible before the timer goes off. Reset the timer, and it is the second student's turn. Students can play against each other by racing to name and match as many letters as they can within two minutes. The winner is the player who names and matches the most letters within the specified time. When students have mastered this level, plastic lowercase letters can replace the uppercase letters in the center of the circle on the board.

Make the Match

Create fifty-two blank cards. On twenty-six of them write the uppercase letters of the alphabet, and on the remaining twenty-six write the lowercase letters. This game may be played individually or with multiple players. You will need the letter cards and a timer. Spread all of the cards face down on the table. Set the timer for two minutes. The student turns the cards over one at a time and names the letters as each card is turned over. The student matches as many of the uppercase letters to the lowercase letters as possible before the timer goes off. If there are multiple players, reset the timer for two minutes and allow the next student to play. The student who matches the most letters before the timer goes off is the winner.

Sound Match

You will need ten to fourteen blank cards, a board, and a timer. Select five to seven phonemes you want to work on with your students. Select two different pictures for each target phoneme, and glue these to the blank cards. Create a board by writing the graphemes that represent each of the selected phonemes in a geometric shape (square, circle, or triangle). Review the names of the pictures just to make sure your students know them. Shuffle the picture cards, and place them face down in a pile between the two players. Set one minute on the timer. The first player will turn over a card and place it on the section of the board that corresponds to the name of its initial consonant phoneme. The player will try to place each card before time is up. A point is earned for each picture correctly placed. The cards will then be shuffled, and the timer reset. The second player will attempt to place more pictures than the first player did in the allotted time. The player with the most points is the winner.

Beat the Clock

Make two copies of the words from the First Grade Dolch Word List, each on a different color so that you have two complete sets of the Dolch list words (see table 5.5). Cut the First Grade Dolch Word Lists into cards. You will need the

Table 5.5   First Grade Dolch Word List

after	has	over
again	her	put
an	him	round
any	his	some
ask	how	stop
as	just	take
by	know	thank
could	let	them
every	live	then
fly	may	think
from	of	walk
give	old	were
going	once	when
had	open	

two sets of words, a timer, and a sheet to record the number of words read correctly. Each student gets one set of words. Set the timer for two minutes. The first student shuffles her words and places them face down in a stack. Start the timer. If the student reads the word correctly, it is put on the table. If a word is read incorrectly, it is placed at the bottom of the pile to be read later. The student reads as many words as possible within the time limit. Then the timer is set for two minutes again. This time, the other student follows the same procedure. After the timer goes off, students count the number of words in their stack of correctly read words. The student with the most cards is the winner. The number of words read correctly by each student is recorded on the sheet.

Treasure Chest

You will need one copy of the Dolch words and the Treasure Chest cards (see figure 5.1). Cut the cards apart and divide the stack evenly, giving half to each student. The students should place their cards in a pile and place the pile in front of them face down on the table. The first student turns over the top card and reads the word. If it is read correctly, the card is placed in the center of the table. If it is incorrect, it is returned to the bottom of the student's stack of cards. The second player turns over the top card, reads it, and places it in the center of the table. When a player turns over a coin card, that student gets to take all the cards that are in the center of the table and places them on the table near the original stack. The game ends when there are no cards left from the original stacks.

always	gave	these
around	goes	those
because	green	upon
been	its	us
before	made	use
best	many	very
both	off	wash
buy	or	which
call	pull	why
cold	read	wish
does	right	work
don't	sing	would
fast	sit	write
first	sleep	your
five	tell	found
their		

Figure 5.1 Treasure Chest Cards.

Then the players count the number of cards they have collected. Any cards left in the center of the table remain there; they are not included in the final count. The student with the most cards at the end of the game is the winner.

Say It Louder!

Give each student a card from the Say It Louder! card set (see figure 5.2). The player who has card number 1 stands and reads the card aloud, emphasizing

1 What will **THEY** do?	**WHAT** will they do?	**2** WHO will make it?
Who will make IT?	**3** WHEN will we go?	When will we GO?
4 **WRITE** it down!	Write **IT** down!	**5** Who will make IT?
WHO will make it?	**6** Did **YOU** see it?	Did you see **IT**?
7 I am certain.	I am Certain.	**8** COULD you go?
Could YOU go?	**9** *USUALLY I am right.*	Usually I am right.
9 We had THEIR dog.	We had their DOG.	**10** When would YOU go?
WHEN would you go?	**11** WHAT did they say?	What did THEY say?

Figure 5.2 Say It Louder Cards.

the word printed in the larger font. The player who has the same statement stands and reads the card aloud, emphasizing the word on the card that is in larger font. The player with card number 2 stands. The play continues until all of the statements have been read.

Encourage the students to discuss how changing the emphasis impacted the meaning of the sentence.

Figure 5.3   Phrase Card.

Find the Phrase

Give each student two different color highlighters and a copy of the phrase card (see figure 5.3). On the phrase card, the phrases have been run together. Individually, students will read each line of text and highlight the phrases in alternating colors. In partners, have students share and compare their highlighting. Students can make changes using a pen to correct any errors in their initial thinking.

Group Them

For this activity you can use any passage. Give each student a copy of a passage that has been formatted so that there are double spaces between each word. Working individually or in pairs, have the students read the text and then draw a line (/) between the words to indicate where they would pause when reading orally. Then have pairs of students orally read the text to each other, making sure to pause at the indicated places in the text.

Radio Announcer

Give students a copy of a short, double-spaced passage they are going to read orally. Students may have either the same or different passages. Tell the students they are going to be radio announcers. It is their job to make a perfect recording of the story so that it can be broadcast on the news. Students record their oral reading of the story individually. Then give each student three different colored pens or pencils. The students then listen to their recordings and on the printed copy place a checkmark above any word omitted, mispronounced, inserted, or that should be read with a different pitch or stress. If there are changes to be made, students record the story a second time. While listening to the second recording, students mark the original copy use a different color. Students mark any areas they are not happy with on the second reading. They then record the passage a final time. This time, students mark any areas they feel are not as well done as they could be in the third color. Using three different colors on the same copy allows students to see their growth while monitoring their reading progress with that particular passage.

Reader's Theater

Reader's theater is an oral performance of a script or story. Students use expression, intonation, and pauses to convey meaning instead of actions or props. The students are not expected to memorize their lines. They only need to read them with expression. Assign a specific character to each student, and give each student a copy of the script. If your students need support with the script, provide read alouds, echo or choral reading, and additional opportunities to practice before they perform the passage. In addition, your students might enjoy adding simple props or costumes and inviting others to attend the performance. During the performance, have the readers stand or sit facing the audience. Videotaping the performance would allow you to share the presentation with an even wider audience.

The Orchestra

Provide each student in the class with the same poem or passage and a highlighter. Ask them to read the passage silently, and highlight words, phrases, or sentences that they find intriguing, powerful, or just fun. The teacher then leads the students through reading the passage aloud. While the teacher is reading orally, each student reads the word, phrase, or sentence they highlighted. Students chime in, keeping pace with the teacher's reading rhythm. Many people might read some sections, while few voices read other sections.

Read Like A . . .

Cut out pictures of people from magazines or write descriptions of various people on cards. Arrange the people cards in one pile, and then create a second set of cards with a short phrase on each card. Each student chooses two cards; the top people card and the top phrase card from each deck. The student reads the fluency phrase card in the way one would expect the person depicted on the people card would say the phrase. The phrases can be constructed to include any vocabulary the class is learning.

REFERENCES

Ardoin, S. P., Witt, J. C., & Suldo, S. M. (2004). Examining the incremental benefits of administering a maze and three versus one curriculum-based measurement reading probes when conducting universal screening. *School Psychology Review, 33,* 218–233.

Carreker, S. (2002). Fluency: No longer a forgotten goal in reading instruction. *Perspectives* (The International Dyslexia Association), *28*(1), 1–4.

Denton, C. A., Barth, A. E., Fletcher, J. M., Wexler, J., Vaughn, S., Cirino, P. T., Romain, M., & Francis, D. J. (2011). The relations among oral and silent reading fluency and comprehension in middle school: Implications for identification and instruction of students with reading difficulties. *Scientific Studies of Reading, 15*(2), 109–135. Retrieved from http://www.ncbi.nlm.nih.gov/pmc/articles/PMC3104321/.

Farstrup, A. E., & Samuels, S. J. (2002). *What Research has to Say about Reading Instruction* (3rd ed.). Newark, DE: International Reading Association.

Fuchs, L. S., Fuchs, D., Hosp, M. K., & Jenkins, J. R. (2001). Oral reading fluency as an indicator of reading competence: A theoretical, empirical, and historical analysis. *Scientific Studies of Reading, 5,* 239–256.

Hosp, M. K., & Fuchs, L. S. (2005). Using CBM as an indicator of decoding, word reading, and comprehension: Do the relations change with grade? *School Psychology Review, 34,* 9–26.

Hudson, R. F., Lane, H. B., & Pullen, P. C. (2005). Reading fluency assessment and instruction: What, why, and how? *The Reading Teacher, 58*(8), 702–714.

Kuhn, M. R., Schwanenflugel, P. J., & Meisinger, E. B. (2010). Aligning theory and assessment of reading fluency: Automaticity, prosody, and definitions of fluency. *Reading Research Quarterly, 45*(2), 230–225.

Kuhn, M. R., & Stahl, S. A. (2003). Fluency: A review of developmental and remedial practices. *Journal of Educational Psychology, 95*(1), 3–21. Retrieved from http://academic.research.microsoft.com/Paper/5773365.aspx.

Learning Point Associates. (2004). *A Closer Look at the Five Essential Components of Effective Reading Instruction: A Review of Scientifically based Reading Research for Teachers.* Retrieved from www.learningpt.org/pdfs/literacy/components.pdf.

National Assessment of Education Progress (NAEP). (2002). *Oral Reading Study.* Washington, DC: U.S. Department of Education National Center for Education Statistics.

National Reading Panel. (2000). *Teaching Children to Read: An Evidence-Based Assessment of the Scientific Research Literature on Reading and its Implications for Reading Instruction.* Retrieved from https://www.nichd.nih.gov/publications/pubs/nrp/Documents/report.pdf.

Pearson Education. (2010). *Elementary Education Guide: Subtest 1.* Amherst, MA: Author.

Pikulski, J. J., & Chard, D. J. (2005). Fluency: Bridge between decoding and reading comprehension. *Reading Teacher, 58*(6), 510–519. Retrieved from http://dx.doi.org.ezproxy.saintleo.edu/10.1598/RT.58.6.2.

Pinnell, G. S., Pikulski, J. J., Wixson, K. K., Campbell, J. R., Gough, P. B., & Beatty, A. S. (1995). *Listening to Children Read Aloud.* Washington, DC: Office of Educational Research and Improvement, U.S. Department of Education.

Reutzel, D. R., & Cooter, R. B. (2011). *Strategies for Reading Assessment and Instruction: Helping Every Child Succeed.* Boston, MA: Pearson.

Tankersley, K. (2003). *Threads of Reading: Strategies for Literacy Development.* Alexandria, VA: Association for Supervision and Curriculum Development.

Truss, L. (2003). *Eats, Shoots & Leaves: The Zero Tolerance Approach to Punctuation.* New York: Gotham.

Wolf, M. (n.d.). New research on an old problem: A brief history of fluency. Retrieved from http://www.scholastic.com/teachers/article/new-research-old-problem-brief-history-fluency.

Chapter 6

Vocabulary

CLASSROOM VISIT

Mrs. Smith begins every Monday with a list of fifteen to twenty vocabulary words for students to copy and define in their science notebooks. She has done this since the beginning of the year, and although students are quiet and working during this activity, she has recently been wondering if they are actually learning the vocabulary words. They do well on the Friday vocabulary quizzes, but she is concerned because she has not seen or heard students using the vocabulary words in their writing or classroom discussions.

Mrs. Smith decided in lieu of a new list of words this Monday, to have a class discussion around the unit of study and the vocabulary words from that unit. She began by explaining to students that she wanted to have a class conversation about the current unit on the food chain, and that every time a vocabulary word was used in the discussion she was going to place a checkmark next to the word listed on the board. First, Mrs. Smith reviewed the vocabulary words by saying each word and asking students to chorally repeat the word so she was sure they were confident in their pronunciation. The words were "consumer," "organisms," "interact," "food web," "predator," "prey," "carnivore," "herbivore," "omnivore," "producer," "transfer," "decomposer," "compete," and "food chain."

She said, "I'm going to begin this discussion with the sentence 'Animals and plants are always involved in a food chain'. Now, it is your turn to build on this comment by using one or more of the vocabulary words listed on the board in the next sentence."

Tatiana raised her hand and said, "Animals have predators." Mrs. Smith smiled and responded, "That is true, Tatiana. Thank you." Mrs. Smith placed a checkmark next to the word "predator." "Can anyone else build on Tatiana's statement using another of the vocabulary words?"

Nelson raised his hand and when called on said, "A tiger is a predator and he eats other animals; those other animals are his prey." Mrs. Smith nodded, placed a checkmark next to the words "prey" and "predator," and said, "That is absolutely correct, Nelson. I think you all have the idea. Let's continue."

Julianne raised her hand and responded, "A tiger might compete with a leopard for the same prey."

"Excellent!" Mrs. Smith said, "Julianne used two of the vocabulary words." She placed a checkmark next to "compete" and "prey." "Let's use all of the words," Mrs. Smith continued, "and remember that you can use a word more than once just like Nelson and Julianne did!" For a long time, the class was silent. Mrs. Smith suggested that students use their vocabulary notebooks. After a few minutes, a hand went up. It was Nathan. "Thank you, Nathan," Mrs. Smith said. Nathan looked at his notebook and said, "An omnanvor is an animal that eats plants and animals."

"That's true," Mrs. Smith responded, "an *omnivore* does eat both plants and animals. Can you use what you just said to add to Julianne's sentence—A tiger might compete with a leopard for the same prey?" Nathan sat silently. "Can anyone use omnivore in a sentence that connects to Julianne's sentence?" she asked. There was no response. "Nathan, you might say, 'An omnivore would be interested in the prey of the leopard and tiger because it eats both meat and plants'. Does that make sense?" Nathan nodded. "Okay, let's continue," she said. The class was silent; no one was willing to offer any additional thoughts. Mrs. Smith decided that tomorrow she would try a different approach.

On Tuesday, Mrs. Smith took the vocabulary words from the food chain unit and began with a cloze activity to see how many of the words the students were able to accurately use. She created a three-paragraph passage on the food chain. Then she deleted the vocabulary words from the passage and replaced them with an underlined space so that the students could place the correct words in the sentences. She provided a word bank of the vocabulary words but included some additional vocabulary words from previous units as well.

After collecting and grading the completed papers, she realized that the results were not good. Even her best science students did not do better than 50 percent accuracy. It was time to take a look at her vocabulary instruction and make some changes!

LITERARY CONNECTION

We're Fearless Flying Hotdogs
We're fearless flying hotdogs,
the famous "Unflappable Five,"
we're mustered in formation
to climb, to dip, to dive,
we spread our wings with relish,
then reach for altitude,
we're aerobatic wieners,
the fastest flying food. (Prelutsky, 2008)

VOCABULARY KNOWLEDGE

Looking at Jack Prelutsky's text, consider the vocabulary: unflappable, mustard, relish, altitude, and aerobatic. These words may be new to students or have a different meaning in the passage from students' current understanding of the word. Although teachers understand the importance of vocabulary in their instruction, they are often at a loss as to how to truly teach it! This text is a perfect example of the significance of understanding multiple meanings for words, and how important it is to understand the context to determine which meaning is being used.

It is estimated that the English language contains somewhere between 450,000 and 750,000 words adapted from a variety of different languages, including Latin, Spanish, French, Greek, and of course Anglo-Saxon English (Tompkins, 2006). Hirsch (2013) indicated that there is a positive correlation between the size of twelfth-grade students' vocabularies and the likelihood of their graduating from college. This seems pretty obvious. The shocking finding was the correlation between twelfth-grade vocabulary and future income level. Hirsch (2013) indicated that studies have established a correlation between vocabulary knowledge and real-world job performance. Vocabulary knowledge is a critical factor in preparing students for college and career readiness.

However, vocabulary knowledge does not just have future benefits; it also has a significant impact on fluency, comprehension, and school success. The National Reading Panel (2000) identified vocabulary as one of the pivotal skills in reading. The increased emphasis on complex informational texts has made developing extensive vocabulary knowledge an even more critical component for teachers to address in their content areas. If decoding skills are well developed, but students are still experiencing difficulty with passage comprehension, the difficulty could be due to a limited understanding of the vocabulary used within the passage. If students do not know 90–95 percent of the vocabulary in the text, they will experience difficulty comprehending it and reading it fluently (Conderman, Hedin, & Bresnahan, 2013).

At first glance, expecting students to know more than 95 percent of the words they read seems high, because as teachers we typically don't aim for 95 percent mastery in other content areas. However, an average page of single-spaced text contains about 500 words. If students know 95 percent of the vocabulary on that page, they would know about 475 of the words. That sounds pretty good. But it also means that for every page of that text that they read, they would not know twenty-five of the words. Those unknown words quickly add up and begin to impact the students' comprehension.

But vocabulary knowledge does not just impact reading comprehension. It can also impact students' abilities to engage in academic classroom discussions, as Ms. Smith discovered. In addition, poorly developed vocabulary skills can make it difficult for students to process new words in oral conversations. Finally, vocabulary development also impacts knowledge acquisition and thought development. Word knowledge provides the cognitive system for systematically storing new information and categorizing it for future use.

TYPES OF VOCABULARY

All of us have four types of vocabulary: listening, speaking, reading, and writing. These four can be combined into two groups, spoken vocabulary and written vocabulary. Spoken vocabulary would include the words used for listening and speaking. These two types begin developing long before school age and form the basis for understanding written language. Written vocabulary would encompass the reading and the writing vocabularies.

Listening vocabulary includes the words we hear and understand orally. This vocabulary knowledge begins at birth or before. Fetuses can detect sounds as early as sixteen weeks (Montgomery, 2007)! From our first days as newborn babies to the day we die, we are listening the whole time we are awake. We are surrounded by spoken vocabulary, whether it is songs we hear, videos we watch, conversations we overhear, or announcers to whom we listen. According to Tompkins (2006), adults typically understand close to 50,000 words. Generally, speaking vocabulary is not as extensively developed as listening vocabulary. Usually, in adults, speaking vocabulary ranges from about 5,000 to 10,000 words. So we do not use all the words we know when speaking.

Reading vocabulary would include those words that you can read and understand in printed form. As adults, this vocabulary tends to be larger than our speaking vocabulary because it only requires that you are able to identify words rather than produce or use these words in context. You do not even need to know the pronunciation! For example, my daughter loved to read and through her reading had been exposed to the word "gauge." Apparently she understood the meaning of the word "gauge" when she read it, but it was not until I actually heard her attempt to use it in conversation that I realized she was mispronouncing it.

During the reading process, the context and usage are provided; you only need to produce the definition, and sometimes the context will help you with that. Consequently, your understanding of a word in print does not need to be as thorough as it does when speaking. Reading vocabulary expands through exposure to a wide variety of printed materials on various topics and genres. As a result, for students who are readers, reading vocabulary tends to be the second-largest vocabulary.

Around third or fourth grade students begin to encounter more words from reading than they do from listening (Duff et al., 2015). If students' reading abilities are lacking, this will have a negative effect on their vocabulary development. Better readers will encounter more uncommon, low-frequency words, and this will have a positive impact on their rate of vocabulary development. Through independent reading experiences, above-average readers' vocabulary will have a higher rate of development than average or below average readers (Duff et al., 2015). If we want students' vocabulary to expand, extensive reading at a variety of levels is necessary. However, it is important for all students to be exposed to grade-level texts no matter what their reading level.

The final type of vocabulary, written vocabulary, encompasses the words that we use to express ourselves in writing. Unlike the other three vocabularies, our written vocabulary is impacted by our ability to spell. Consequently, our spelling ability has an impact on the words that we use to express our thoughts. Perhaps you have experienced this. Have you ever chosen a different word when you were writing because you were not sure how to spell the first one you thought of using?

The average six-year-olds begin first grade with a spoken vocabulary of about 8,000 words. They then learn about 3,000 to 5,000 words per year (Senechal & Cornell, 1993). Consequently, effective vocabulary instruction needs to begin early and continue throughout the school years (Nagy, 2005). However, it has been estimated that teachers can only directly teach about 400 words a year (Montgomery, 2007). The rest of these words need to be learned through incidental exposure in the students' environment whether overheard casually or read in printed material. The National Institute of Child Health and Human Development (2000) found that children learn the meaning of most words indirectly through everyday experiences with oral and written language. This acquisition could happen directly through conversations, indirectly by being read to, or through their own independent reading.

VOCABULARY TIERS

So, if you only have time to teach about 400 words a year, or about 10 words a week, or approximately 60 words from each content area, how do you choose which words to teach? Beck, McKeown, and Kucan (2008) developed a model for categorizing vocabulary into tiers. They describe three levels, or tiers, of words based on the word's frequency and applicability of use. The Common Core State Standards also reference these three tiers of words (Rhodus, 2012). The Common Core State Standards Initiative explained Tier One words as those words that are basic and/or concrete and would generally be used in conversation. These would be the words that you would expect most students at a specific grade level to be familiar with orally, even if they do not recognize them in print. These would include words such as "table" or "box."

Tier Two words can also be referred to as general academic words. These words are more abstract but could be used in various content areas. They have general utility across content areas. These would include words like "surface" and "avoided."

Tier Three words are those that are highly specialized and tend to be subject specific. These words are generally only used in one content area and do not occur as frequently. Tier Three words would include words like "isotope" and "ukulele."

In your teaching focus on providing instruction for Tier Two words and providing immediate support for understanding Tier Three words. Tier Two words require more extensive instruction so that the student is able to know and remember them, while Tier Three words typically only require the definition to be taught (Rhodus, 2012). To determine if a word is a Tier Two or Tier Three word, ask yourself these three questions. First, is this a generally useful word? Next, does the word relate to other words and ideas that students know or have been learning? And, finally, is the word useful in helping students understand the specific text and is it applicable in other content areas? If you can answer yes to all three questions, then it is probably a Tier Two word rather than a Tier Three word.

Marzano and Pickering (2005) identified the following eight research-based characteristics of effective vocabulary instruction. (1) Vocabulary instruction should not only focus on the definition of the word. (2) Students should have the opportunity to represent their understanding of the word using both linguistic and nonlinguistic methods. (3) Students should have multiple exposures to the word so that they understand its use in a variety of settings. (4) Students should develop an understanding of the morphological units within the word. (5) Not all words should be taught in the same way. Different words may fit better within certain types of instruction. Teachers should match the instruction to the word. (6) Students should have opportunities to use the word in discussions with others. (7) Word play is important. Students need to have multiple opportunities to engage with words. (8) Instruction needs to focus on those words students will see more frequently to ensure that students can use these words to impact their academic success.

Some suggestions for implementing effective vocabulary instruction would be to increase independent reading time, use read alouds to expose students to higher-level vocabulary, discuss unknown words, keep vocabulary instruction interactive, use the vocabulary frequently in various situations, and incorporate graphic organizers.

VOCABULARY ASSESSMENT

Assessing vocabulary knowledge is more difficult than assessment in the previous strands we have discussed because, unlike phonological awareness, phonics, and fluency, vocabulary knowledge is multidimensional and continues to develop throughout your lifetime. Paris (2005), in his discussion of the pillars of reading development, explained that phonological awareness, phonics, and fluency were constrained and developed linearly. He further explained that students tended to master these skills within a specific period of time. However, vocabulary and comprehension were unconstrained and as such did not lend themselves as easily to individual assessments. Understanding of the shades of meaning and the connotation of words continues to develop even after the specific definition of a vocabulary word is learned.

Informal

The National Reading Panel found that teacher-generated assessments of vocabulary knowledge that matched instruction would be more effective in determining vocabulary growth as compared to standardized vocabulary assessments (National Institute of Child Health and Human Development, 2000). In fact, rather than focusing strictly on formal assessments, vocabulary assessments can be completed informally through classroom observation. If you have concerns about a student's vocabulary development, you could choose a passage in which you would expect the student to know 90–95 percent of the words. The student may experience frustration reading passages where less than 90 percent of the words are known because not enough information is obtained from the passage for adequate comprehension. As the student is reading the passage, record the words that were difficult for the student. Analyze this list and begin direct vocabulary instruction with the Tier Two words with which the student experienced difficulty.

Cloze Tests

Sometimes you may want to determine vocabulary knowledge of a larger group of students on a specific topic where there is not time for each student to read the passage orally, as Ms. Smith did earlier in this chapter. Cloze tests can be an effective way to use a content-based passage to assess whole-group vocabulary knowledge. A cloze test is constructed using a short passage approximately a page in length, from content you have taught or that you will be using for instruction. Constructing a cloze test is relatively simple. Choose or compose a passage of about 250 to 500 words. You will want to make sure to keep the first sentence complete to help establish the context for the passage; do not delete any words from the first sentence. Beginning with the second sentence of the passage, choose one of the first five words of that second sentence to delete. Replace that word with a blank. Then delete every fifth word after the blank until you have about fifty blanks. Make sure to finish the cloze assessment with a complete sentence. Again, the complete sentences at the beginning and end of the passage help to provide the context for the student.

The students must then read the passage and provide a word that would make sense in each blank in the passage. In order for students to get credit for a word they supply, it must be the exact word from the original passage. The goal is for students to comprehend the passage to the extent that they can match the author's voice, tone, and word choice. This can be a difficult process so typically there are many errors, but misspelling should not be counted as incorrect. Do not be alarmed if the students do not score particularly well because to demonstrate proficiency a high percentage correct score is not needed. The passage is considered to be at students' independent level if they score at least 50 percent correct. It would be at the instructional level if the students score between 33 and 49 percent correct. If the students score below 32 percent correct, the students would have scored at the frustration level for this passage. But just knowing the percentage correct score is not enough. Examining recurring class errors would provide information about the vocabulary words that the students need to master. You would want to teach these words explicitly during whole-group instruction.

Maze Tests

If you think students might find a passage particularly difficult, you might want to construct a maze test instead of a cloze test. A maze test provides more scaffolding for students. When creating a maze, follow the same procedure for constructing a cloze test; however, this time, provide three choices for each deleted word. One choice would be the correct word, the second would be an incorrect word that is the same part of speech, and the third choice would be an incorrect word that is a different part of speech. Because the words are provided, the scoring levels for the maze test are different. For the independent level, students must answer 85 percent or more of the choices correctly. For the instructional level, they must answer 50 to 84 percent correctly; and for the frustration level, they would have answered less than 49 percent correctly (Reutzel & Cooter, 2011). Cloze and maze assessments can provide specific information about reading vocabulary in a certain context or content area.

Written Vocabulary Knowledge Assessments

It might be helpful to also obtain information about students' written vocabulary knowledge. Assessing vocabulary through writing provides teachers with information about written vocabulary development. In attempting to obtain this information, it is usually more effective to have students write about an idea they have discussed rather than just having them compose a cold response to a writing prompt. You might read a short passage to the class and then allow the students to talk about their observations with a shoulder partner. You could then provide five minutes for each student to write more extensively about one specific observation they made about the passage that was read. To score this type of written vocabulary assessment, count the number of mature words (eight or more letters) that the student uses in his written response. If the student has misspelled the word, still count this word if the correct spelling has eight or more letters. Using this type of assessment throughout the year would enable you to monitor written vocabulary growth (Conderman, Hedin, & Bresnahan, 2013).

Vocabulary Knowledge Scales

Knowing a word is not typically an all-or-nothing situation. With each additional exposure to a word, your understanding of the meaning tends to expand. Dale (1965) initially described word knowledge in four stages. The first stage would be no exposure to the term. The second stage would include being aware of the word but not knowing what it means. The third stage would be having a vague understanding of the word. The fourth and final stage he described was knowing the word and remembering it. However, Beck, McKeown, and Omanson (1987) further developed the continuum to include five stages. The first would be no knowledge of the word. The second would be a general understanding. The third would an ability to recognize the meaning based on one specific context. The fourth would be knowing the word but being unable to recall it enough to use it in speech or writing. The final stage would be the ability to use the word in various situations. Both descriptions illustrate the continuum of vocabulary knowledge.

Vocabulary assessments may be used to measure the breadth or depth of vocabulary knowledge. The maze and cloze assessments tend to measure vocabulary breadth. Vocabulary depth refers to how much students know about the specific word. The Vocabulary Knowledge Scale (Stahl & Bravo, 2010) is an informal assessment that attempts to measure both reading and writing vocabularies in a more multifaceted setting and is aligned with Dale's (1965) and Beck et al.'s (1987) stages of vocabulary knowledge. Students are given a list of words and are asked to rate their knowledge of the words. Students can earn between one and five points for each word. They earn one point if they do not remember having seen the word before; two points if they have seen the word but don't know what it means; three points if they have seen the word and think they can provide a synonym or definition; four points if they know the word and can give a correct synonym or definition; and five points if they can use the word correctly in a sentence (Stahl & Bravo, 2010).

Vocabulary instruction is not a simple process. We have learned that looking up words and defining them from the dictionary is not a best practice. When using the dictionary, students often have difficulty determining which meaning matches the context in which the word was used, and they are typically only exposed to one meaning. Finding the word in the dictionary also does not provide enough opportunities for repeated exposure and independent use. Words are learned through explicit instruction, extensive reading, repeatedly hearing the words being used, and multiple opportunities for their usage in context. Vocabulary knowledge is one of the many keys to comprehension, and we need to provide students with the strategies necessary for making unknown words understandable so they can comprehend what they are reading, which is the final goal of any reading activity.

VOCABULARY ACTIVITIES

Snowball Fight

Divide your group of students into pairs. Assign each pair of students one vocabulary word, and provide them with two pieces of 8½" × 11" paper. On one paper, they are to write the word in large letters, and, if applicable, they are to underline the base or the root, circle any prefixes, and box any suffixes. On the second paper, they are to write the definition of the word in their own words. Explain to the students that they are going to participate in a snowball fight. Instruct the pairs of students to crumple the papers into a ball. This will be their "snowball." When you give the signal, they are to throw the crumpled vocabulary "snowball" at someone across the room. They are to then pick a "snowball" up off the floor and continue tossing the snowballs until the teacher signals everyone to stop after about five to ten seconds.

After the signal to stop is given, each student picks up one snowball and unwraps it. The students will then mingle in an attempt to find the match for the word or definition on their papers. When they find the person who has the definition or word that matches with the information on their snowball, the pair collaborates and creates a sentence using the word in context. Students then share out their words, definitions, and sentences. As a variation, students can share out their definitions, and the class can respond by writing the word on a whiteboard or sheet of paper.

Race to the Apex!

Prepare two pyramids with vocabulary from the current unit of instruction, similar to the one pictured in figure 6.1. Divide students into pairs. One student, the clue guesser, sits with his back to the board where the pyramid will be projected, while the clue giver faces the board where the pyramid will be projected. When they are settled, the teacher projects the pyramid. The teacher says "begin," and the clue giver starts at the bottom of pyramid giving clues for the first word on the bottom left. When the clue guesser says the word, the clue giver moves onto the next word and works his way up the

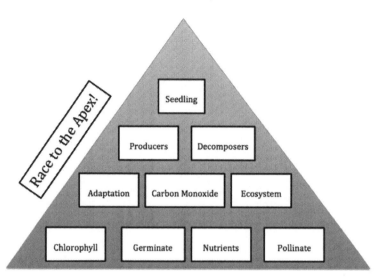

Figure 6.1   Race to the Apex!

pyramid. The clue giver may not use the actual word or any form of the word in his clues. When he reaches the top and all of the words have been guessed, the pair stands, indicating that they are done. When the whole class is standing or the given time is up, the students trade places and the teacher projects the next set of words. Play continues in the same manner for round 2.

Word Sorts

Word sorts can be open or closed. In both constructs, word sorts support connections among vocabulary terms and critical thinking about vocabulary terms. In an open word sort, the teacher provides a list of vocabulary words to students who are working individually, in pairs, or in small groups. Students organize the words into groups and determine a name for each of the groups. This will provide opportunities for the students to organize the information and help with the retrieval of the definitions.

In a closed word sort, students are given a list of vocabulary words related to a specific topic and are given categories in which to sort them. Often a category for Unknown Words is also included. Word sorts can also be used as pre- and posttests to determine students' understanding of vocabulary prior to and/or at the conclusion of a unit of study. This can provide specific data related to vocabulary growth within a unit of study.

Autumn Leaves

Divide students into small groups. Provide each group of students with a poster paper illustration of a leafless tree with branches. On the trunk you need to write a root or base word. Each group of students should have a different root or base word. Give students five to ten minutes to brainstorm examples of words containing the given root or base. As students think of a word, they should draw a leaf on the trees and write the word inside the leaf. Each student in the group should have the same color marker. For example, students could be given the root word "cycl." This would be written on the trunk of the tree. The teacher could also provide information about its Greek origin and its meaning. "Cylc" means circular. Students might write the words *bicycle*, *cycle*, and *cyclone* on the leaves. After the predetermined time limit, perhaps ten minutes, the student groups should then rotate through the other posters, spending three to five minutes at each poster and adding leaves with any additional appropriate words. The new group of students should have a different color marker to create the "autumn" leaves effect. This will allow the teacher to determine which words were created or added by which group of students. When students are rotating through the posters, you may also want to allow students to use electronic devices or dictionaries to find additional words.

Seven Most Important Words

Prior to your unit of instruction, ask pairs of students to brainstorm what they think the most important words for the unit might be. After two to three minutes, ask students to agree upon and circle what they think will be the seven most important of these words and to provide a written rationale for selecting those particular words. After your lesson, ask students to revisit their list of words and revise it based on the new information that they have learned (adapted from Bleich, 1975).

Frayer Puzzles

Frayers are terrific graphic organizers for large concept words such as "racism," "freedom," and "compassion." Have each student create a Frayer organizer by folding a piece of 8½" × 11" paper in quarters and then folding down the upper left-hand corner of the folded square to form a small triangle in each quarter. Your unfolded finished organizer should resemble a paper with four quadrants and a diamond in the center between the quadrants.

You will need paper, scissors, and an envelope. In the center diamond, the students write their target concept word. In the upper left quadrant, students write a definition of the concept in their own words; in the upper right quadrant, students name characteristics, features, or qualities of the concept; in the lower left-hand quadrant, students give examples of the concept; and finally, in the lower right quadrant, students should provide non-examples of the concept. Students then cut along the folded lines between the quadrants and diamond. This divides the paper into puzzle pieces.

Arrange the students in pairs or small groups Each student in the group places their puzzle pieces in the same envelope so there are at least two puzzles in one envelope, and the envelope is then shared with a second grouping of students who reassemble the Frayer models in the envelope they are given. Students then check each other's work (Frayer, n.d.).

Conversation Vocabulary

Post your vocabulary words in the room where they are visible to all students. Explain that you want to have a conversation about your recent unit of study and that students will be expected to use the vocabulary words listed on the board as they discuss the topic. Choose one student to be the recorder, and every time a word is used, the student places a check next to that word. Students will need to listen to one another's comments and build on them. Model the process for students so they have an idea of your expectations. For example, if the words were "protagonist," "antagonist," "character," "climax," "rising action," "falling action," "resolution," "exposition," or "theme," you might begin your conversation with "Maniac Magee is one of my favorite 'protagonists' ever." You would then place a checkmark next to the word protagonist. A second sentence might be, "One of the reasons he is my favorite 'character' is because of all the things he did to become a legend—like untying the Cobble's Knot." Then you would place a checkmark next to the word "character."

An extension to this activity is that while the students are giving their responses, the teacher could type and project students' contributions to the conversation. Placing students' initials or names next to their contributions can be very motivating for students. The conversation can continue until time expires or the conversation dwindles.

Homophone Match

The teacher writes a set of homophones on the board, for example, "tail" and "tale." Then the teacher provides a definition for one of the words, for example, "The back part of an animal that is flexible enough to wag." Students then choose the correct homophone and write it on their individual whiteboards. This encourages all students to be involved in the activity, rather than just calling on one student.

An alternate activity would be for the teacher to provide one word from a set of homophones, for example, "bawl," and two definitions such as "To cry loudly" or "A spherical shape used in games." The students must choose the correct definition that matches the printed homophone.

Multiple-Meaning Word Spoons

Create several sets of twenty-eight blank cards. For this activity, the teacher will need to choose seven words that have multiple meanings. Divide the set of cards into seven groups of three. For each of the seven words, complete three cards. On one card write the word, on the second card write the first definition, and on the third card write a second definition. Divide students into small groups. Give each group of students a copy of the deck of cards and one less spoon than the number of students in the group. For example, if there are four students in the group, there should be three spoons. Place the spoons in the center of the table so they are in reach of all players.

The object of the game is to be the first player to match a multiple-meaning word with two correct meanings of the word, creating a set of three cards (see figure 6.2). When a player has a matched set, he grabs or sneaks a spoon from

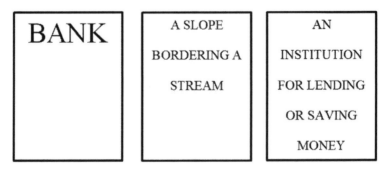

Figure 6.2 Multiple Meaning Word Spoons.

the center of the table. Only a player with a matching set of cards can grab the spoon first, and then every other player must quickly try to grab a spoon for himself. The player who does not get a spoon gets the first letter in the word spoons, "s," and the play continues with the student next to the original dealer beginning the second round. If the same person does not get a spoon during the second round, he gets the letter "p." The game ends when time is up. The person who has the least amount of letters is the winner.

To begin play, the dealer shuffles the cards and passes out five cards to each player. The dealer places the deck of remaining cards in a pile face down on the table and selects the top card. He looks at the card and decides if he wants to keep it or pass it. If he wants to keep it, he passes one of the cards from his hand of five cards to the next player in a clockwise direction. The play continues in that way around the table. The last player starts the discard pile. If the players go through the whole deck before the game ends, the discard pile is turned over and used.

Sticking Together

At the end of a unit of study, students are organized into groups of four. Each group gets a set of sticky notes and a piece of chart paper divided into four sections. Students write one vocabulary word from the unit on each sticky note. The group of students then work together to categorize the words into the four different sections. The group members decide on a title for each section that illustrates why they think those particular words should stick together. The first group to logically categorize the vocabulary words is the winner.

Quick Draw

The class is divided into four teams. Each team is given a whiteboard, a marker, and an eraser. Within each team, the members number off. Each of the students will have a turn based upon their number. The team member who is number one should have the whiteboard and the marker. The teacher tells the class the first vocabulary word. When the teacher says "go," the first student will draw a picture that depicts the meaning of the word. Team members may help as needed. One point is awarded to each team who illustrates the word correctly. The whiteboard is then passed to the next student who draws a picture for the next word. Play continues until all vocabulary words are illustrated. Each team gets one point for each correctly drawn picture to represent the meaning of the word. The team with the most points at the end of the game wins.

Eye Spy

The teacher creates a list of the new vocabulary words and determines a point value for each word depending on the number of syllables, frequency use, and clearness of contextual definitions. Students have a predetermined amount of time to search the text to find each new word. On a sheet of paper students write the page and paragraph number where the word is located. Then they examine the context and write down what they believe to be the definition of the new word based on the context.

Linear Array

Students create a graphic organizer with a rectangle, three ovals, and then another rectangle in a single line going from left to right across the paper. The new vocabulary word is written in the rectangle on the far left. The opposite of the word is written in the rectangle on the far right. The students then fill in the center three ovals with words that are gradually less similar until they reach the opposite. For example, given the five words "enormous," "tiny," "petite," "microscopic," and "large" students could complete the linear array by placing "microscopic" and "enormous" in each of the rectangles. The words "tiny," "petite," and "large" would be arranged in the three ovals between the two rectangles in the order from left to right "tiny," "petite," and "large."

Wheel of Fortune

The teacher creates a spinner to use for this game. The spaces on the spinner are labeled with such choices as the following: "Draw It!" "Act It Out!" "Give an Antonym," "Define It!" and "Use It in a Sentence." All of the words are placed in a bag. The student chooses a word from the bag and spins the spinner. If he is able to complete the indicated activity correctly, he gets one point. The student with the most points at the end of the game wins. This activity can also be modified to be a team competition.

REFERENCES

Beck, I. L., McKeown, M. G., & Kucan, L. (2002). *Bringing Words to Life: Robust Vocabulary Instruction.* New York: Guilford Press.

Beck, I. L., McKeown, M. G., & Omanson, R. C. (1987). The effects and uses of diverse vocabulary instructional techniques. In M. C. McKeown, & M. E. Curtis (Eds.), *The Nature of Vocabulary Acquisition* (pp. 147–163). Hillsdale, NJ: Erlbaum.

Bleich, D. (1975). *Reading and Feelings: An Introduction to Subjective Criticism.* Urbana, IL: National Council of Teachers of English.

Conderman, G., Hedin, L., & Bresnahan, V. (2013). *Strategy Instruction for Middle and Secondary Students with Mild Disabilities.* Thousand Oaks, CA: Corwin. Retrieved from http://www.sagepub.com/upm-data/54582_Conderman_Ch_3.pdf.

Dale, E. (1965). Vocabulary measurement: Techniques and major findings. *Elementary English, 42*(8), 895–901.

Duff, D., Tomblin, J. B., & Catts, H. (2015, June). The influence of reading on vocabulary growth: A case for a Matthew Effect. *Journal of Speech, Language, and Hearing Research, 58*(3): 853–864. doi: 10.1044/2015_JSLHR-L-13-0310.

Hirsch, E. D. (2013). A wealth of words. *City Journal.* Retrieved from http://www.city-journal.org/2013/23_1_vocabulary.html.

Marzano, R. J., & Pickering, D. J. (2005). *Building Academic Vocabulary: Teacher's Manual.* Alexandria, VA: ASCD.

Montgomery, J. K. (2007). *The Bridge of Vocabulary: Evidence Activities for Academic Success.* Boston: Pearson. Retrieved from http://www.srsdeaf.org/Downloads/Bridge_of_Vocabulary.pdf.

National Institute of Child Health and Human Development. (2000). *The Report of the National Reading Panel: Teaching Children to Read: An Evidence-Based Assessment of the Scientific Research Literature on Reading and its Implications for Reading Instruction: Reports of the Subgroups.* Washington, DC: U.S. Government Printing Office. Retrieved from http://www.nationalreadingpanel.org.

Paris, S. G. (2005). Reinterpreting the development of reading skills. *Reading Research Quarterly, 40*(2), 184–202. Retrieved from http://onlinelibrary.wiley.com/doi/10.1598/RRQ.40.2.3/abstract.

Prelutsky, J. (2008). *Pizza, Pigs, and Poetry: How to Write a Poem.* New York: Greenwillow Books.

Reutzel, D. R., & Cooter, R. B. (2011). *Strategies for Reading Assessment and Instruction: Helping Every Child Succeed.* Boston: Pearson.

Rhodus, K. (2012). Vocabulary instruction and the Common Core. *Creative Commons Attribution.* Retrieved from http://www.aea267.k12.ia.us/system/assets/uploads/files/76/which_words_to_teach.pdf.

Stahl, K. A., & Bravo, M. A. (2010). Contemporary classroom vocabulary assessments for content areas. *The Reading Teacher, 63*(7), 566–578. Retrieved from http://steinhardt.nyu.edu/scmsAdmin/uploads/006/716/Stahl%20Voc%20Assess%20RT.pdf.

Tompkins, G. E. (2006). *Literacy for the 21st Century: A Balanced Approach* (4th ed.). Boston: Pearson.

Chapter 7

Comprehension

CLASSROOM VISIT

As students sat reading silently, Mrs. Johnson called Cory over to her table for a reading conference. Cory puzzled her. He was one of those students who sounded like a good reader but did poorly on both classroom and state reading assessments. Cory came over with his book, *The Lightning Thief*, in his hand.

"How do you like this book, Cory?" she asked.

"It's okay. But you know, I really don't like to read," he said.

This was not the first time Mrs. Smith heard him say this, so she decided to address it head-on. "What don't you like about reading, Cory?"

"It's boring," he replied.

"What else do you not like about reading?" she asked.

"When I read, I can't remember anything," he responded.

That made sense. It was obvious that when reading, he was saying the words but not doing the mental work necessary to actively engage with the text.

"Let's talk about some things you can do to help you remember what you read, Cory. I'm going to teach you a million-dollar word. The word is meta-cognition. Can you repeat it?"

"Meta-cog-nition," he repeated.

"It means to be aware of what you are thinking about. You need to think about the text as you read it. Sometimes when I have no idea what I've read,

I realize that I was thinking about something else. Maybe I was thinking about something my daughter said to me or about something I have to do after school, but I was not thinking about what I was reading. Have you ever read something and when you get to the end, you realized you had no idea what you just read?"

"Yes," he said looking down at his book.

"What do you do when that happens?" Mrs. Smith asked.

"I sometimes read it again," he replied.

"That's a great strategy; does that help?" asked Mrs. Smith.

"Sometimes," Cory stated.

"Well, I am going to give you some strategies in addition to rereading the text that might help you remember it better. Take out your reading goal sheet. Let's talk about what we are going to try first. When you are reading a story, it is important to make connections to what you are reading. It might be a connection to something you already know or something else you have read. Show me where you are in your book." Cory opened his book to the page he had been reading. "Good, let's read this page aloud, and I'll show you what I do in my head to understand and remember what I read; then we'll let you try it." Mrs. Smith began reading and paused occasionally to let Cory know what she was thinking about as she read the page.

LITERARY CONNECTION

It wasn't that I hated being asked a bunch of questions. I had nothing against questions. I just didn't like listening to them, because some questions take forever to make sense. Sometimes waiting for a question to finish is like watching someone draw an elephant starting with the tail first. As soon as you see the tail your mind wanders all over the place and you think of a million other animals that also have tails until you don't care about the elephant because it's only one thing when you've been thinking about a million others. (Gantos, 2011, p. 34)

Comprehension is the ultimate goal of any reading activity. If students can pronounce the words in the text and read them fluently with expression, but don't understand, the "reading" was pointless. The purpose of providing instruction in the other strands of reading—phonological awareness, phonics, vocabulary, and fluency—is to build students' automaticity in the mechanics of the reading process so that comprehension can occur. However, sometimes even though students appear to be able to "read" the text, they do not understand it, as illustrated in our classroom scenario. In this case, more instruction in the basic skills is not enough. Students must recognize that they need to be thinking when they are reading, and that thinking about the text is what readers do (Harvey & Goudvis, 2017). Students must also develop strategies for constructing meaning at the literal, inferential, and critical levels.

FACTORS THAT IMPACT COMPREHENSION

Snow (2002) defined comprehension as the process of "simultaneously extracting and constructing meaning through interaction and involvement with written language" (p. 11). In other words, the text is important, but it is not the only factor that impacts understanding. Comprehension occurs as the result of the combination of three factors within a specific setting: the reader, the text, and the activity. These three factors are situated within a specific sociocultural context. This context can impact comprehension. We have discussed the triad of text complexity in chapter 1, but Snow (2002) also identified factors outside of text complexity that can impact comprehension.

Reader

The first factor to consider is the reader. Among other skills, the reader must possess cognitive abilities such as attention, memory, critical analysis, and the ability to make inferences. These need to accompany linguistic, domain, and topic knowledge. Phonological awareness, phonics, vocabulary, and fluency can provide the foundation for comprehension, and well-developed skills in these areas can also help to improve comprehension. Fluent, expressive reading of the text usually requires comprehension of the ideas expressed. Quick efficient word recognition and knowledge of grammar and mechanics are necessary for fluent reading. Vocabulary knowledge is necessary for comprehension; however, comprehension of the text can expand vocabulary knowledge through exposure to new words in context. Noncognitive reader factors such as interest and motivation can also impact comprehension. These noncognitive factors may increase or decrease depending on positive or negative experiences with the text.

It is important to consider the impact of the readers' interests and prior knowledge on comprehension. In 1988 Recht and Leslie conducted an investigation of the effect of prior knowledge on comprehension in what has become known as the Baseball Study. The study was conducted with thirty-two seventh-grade and thirty-two eighth-grade students from an urban middle school. The data from the participants were analyzed in four groups. These were students with a high reading ability and an extensive knowledge of baseball, students with a high reading ability and little knowledge of baseball, students with a low reading ability and an extensive knowledge of baseball, and students with a low reading ability and a little knowledge of baseball. As might be expected, the students with high reading ability and extensive knowledge of baseball performed the best on the comprehension assessment, but more notably, the low reading ability students with an extensive knowledge of baseball significantly outperformed the students with high reading ability and little knowledge of baseball. Recht and Leslie (1988) stated that "knowledge of a content domain is a powerful determinant of the amount and quality of information recalled, powerful enough for poor readers to compensate for their generally low reading ability" (p. 19).

You will remember that in chapter 1, we explained the impact of culture and personal experience on literacy development as determined in a similar study about wedding ceremonies. What conclusions can we draw from both of these studies? When considering the reader, we must consider the impact their prior knowledge will have on the comprehension of the specific text.

Text

The features of the text itself can impact comprehension. These text features could include headings, subheadings, photographs, captions, bold or italic print, maps, timelines, glossaries, tables of contents, sidebars, and bulleted lists, just to name a few. Each of these can help students organize the information within the text and assists them in retaining it. When authors use these features, they are attempting to create considerate texts that have clear text structures or patterns of organization. In addition, the use of headings, transition words, and directly stated main ideas creates coherency of the text which helps support comprehension. Considerate texts may provide support through prereading questions, vocabulary aids, and/or activities (McGraw-Hill,

2005). However, not all texts are considerate or are meant to be considerate. Teachers need to be aware of the type of text they are using. Some texts will require more teacher scaffolding than others. Another often-overlooked factor of considerate text would be the amount of white space on the page. This white space includes both the spacing between the lines and the spacing around the print (Doty, Cameron, & Barton, 2003).

Texts come in many different varieties, fonts, sizes, and formats. They could be print or digital, narrative or informational, lexical or pictorial, easy or difficult. The ever-increasing inundation of digital media has expanded our definition of what constitutes text. Texts are no longer just print-based books or articles. Digital texts now encompass an ever-expanding array of eBooks, websites, videos, text messages, and social media. The nonlinear arrangement of information on digital pages through hyperlinks and graphics may present challenges, while providing additional support for comprehension (Snow, 2002). The combination of print and electronic media within a single source, such as in the novel *Skeleton Creek* (Carmen, 2009), where links and passwords take you to video recordings that are necessary to understand the story, may present benefits and challenges to the comprehension process.

We tend to classify texts as either narrative or informational, but in reality texts can be placed anywhere along the continuum from narrative to informational. A text may be totally informational, such as an encyclopedia entry, or totally narrative, such as a novel. However, texts can also contain both narrative and informational features, as illustrated by *The Magic School Bus* (Cole, 1990) series or *The Diary of a Young Girl* (Frank, 1952). Both factual information and a narrative are combined to convey each book's message.

Texts can be arranged along a continuum from lexical to pictorial. In some picture books, the story is conveyed completely by the pictures with little or no text, such as the book *Good Dog, Carl* by Day (1996). At the other end of the continuum, there are many chapter books that contain no pictures other than perhaps the one on the front cover. Books could be located anywhere along this continuum.

The passage's position on the readability continuum from easy to hard is often the most frequently considered factor. The readability of a text would include its actual reading or grade-level appropriateness as determined by the vocabulary and sentence complexity. However, readability is further impacted by the content and ideas within the text itself.

Reader and the Text

Readability is impacted not only by the reader and the text but also by the purpose or goal of the reading activity. Generally, there are three main purposes for reading a text: increasing knowledge, such as with an informational text; applying information, such as repairing a dishwasher; or entertaining, such as reading a novel (Snow, 2002).

The reader, the text, and the activity all occur within a specific sociocultural context. Typically, as teachers, the context we think of is the classroom; however, classrooms are made up of children who come to the reading experience with different capabilities and experiences, which are influenced by their home, neighborhood, culture, and physical environment. Vygotsky (1978) stressed the importance of the more knowledgeable teacher providing support for learners as they master new skills. These supports are gradually removed as independence is achieved. Vygotsky's view stressed the equal importance of three factors: the way the instruction is delivered, the social interactions involved in the experience, and the content itself. As we discovered from the Baseball Study, we must also consider the knowledge of students. Flexibility with a student's text level may be necessary based on the topic and the student's knowledge.

Text sets can be used to support comprehension of texts that are challenging. A text set includes a complex anchor text and additional texts on the topic that support the anchor text. The additional texts may be at a less complex, more comfortable level to scaffold the reader's knowledge and build confidence (Glasswell & Ford, 2010). In addition to written texts, a text set can include videos, graphics, maps, photos, and other artifacts. Text sets should be intentionally sequenced in complexity and cognitive load to build knowledge and vocabulary (Garrison, 2016).

Tharp and Gallimore (1988) identified five sociocultural characteristics that impact literacy: the participants, how the activity is defined, the timing of the activity, where it occurs, and children's motivation for being involved in the activity. Oftentimes we are more motivated to participate in an activity in one environment than we are in another. I accomplish significantly more reading in my easy chair at home than I do sitting at my desk at work. Even though the activity is the same, my mental state and ability to concentrate are better at home. When I am physically comfortable and mentally relaxed, I comprehend the material more easily. The same tends to be true for our students. Classroom environment plays an important role in students' motivation to read and in their willingness to persevere with more challenging texts.

COMPREHENSION SKILLS AND STANDARDS

The goal of education is to prepare students to be successful in college and career. Research by the Common Core State Standards Initiative indicated that over the past fifty years, the text complexity at the college and career levels has been consistent or even increased, while the textual complexity used within K–12 schools has decreased especially at the secondary level (Hiebert, 2012a). In an attempt to close the gap between reading materials used in the K–12 setting and those used in college and career settings, the Lexile grade-level bands for text complexity have been recalculated (Hiebert, 2012b). Consequently, one of the key shifts in language arts is that the expected text difficulty and complexity recommended for use at each grade level have increased.

Reading comprehension involves a variety of skills. Carlisle and Rice (2002) explain that adept readers decode words, rapidly and accurately, attach meaning to words and sentences, connect the new information to prior knowledge that is pertinent, create and maintain mental representations or visual images of what they have read, predict or hypothesize what is to come, and make decisions about the purpose for reading—all at the same time. We would argue that that is just the tip of the iceberg.

If we look at the Common Core standards for comprehension of text, students are expected to do so much beyond what Carlisle and Rice (2002) indicated. The Common Core reading anchor standards are organized into three large categories or clusters each containing three anchor standards. These three major categories include "the main idea and details of the text," "the craft and structure the author uses within the text," and "the integration of knowledge and ideas within and among texts" (Common Core State Standards Initiative, 2014a).

The main idea and details category would include understanding of explicitly stated ideas and logical inferences, the development of central themes, and how individuals, ideas, and events develop throughout the text. The "craft and structure" category includes the understanding of words and phrases, that is, when we mentioned the tip of the iceberg previously, you determined whether we meant this literally or figuratively; the analysis of the structure of phrases, sentences, and longer sections; and understanding the effect of the author's point of view or purpose on the text. The final category, "integration of knowledge and ideas within and among texts," includes evaluation of content in diverse media and formats, evaluation of arguments and claims, and analysis within, between, and among texts (Calkins, Ehrenworth, & Lehman, 2012). Scaffolding students by providing instruction across each of the three major categories will help develop the skills needed to critically analyze and synthesize information within, between, and among print and digital text and media.

Carlisle and Rice (2002) point out that reading involves a multitude of synchronous actions that facilitate comprehension. When students read a text, it is important for them to determine the main idea and details that are central to the understanding of the text. When students read, they should be asking themselves: What does the author want us to know and how does the author go about conveying this?

Determining the main idea and details supports the comprehension of the text. However, placing all of the learning focus on one standard does not support comprehension of the entire text. For example, recently I was visiting an eighth-grade class. Students were completing a text structure graphic organizer for the text they were reading. They readily and accurately were able to tell me about the structure of the text, but when asked what the text was about, what the author wanted them to know from reading the text, they were unable to answer that question. It is important to encourage teachers to have students read the text the first time to determine the author's message, the core understandings, or the key ideas of the text. The second time students read, they are better prepared to analyze the textual components. Often this read is for the purpose of determining how the author delivered the message. This second read is where the standards come into play. Questions such as the following would be appropriate: How did the structure of the poem contribute to the meaning of the text? How did the characters change as the plot moved toward a resolution?

Teaching standards and skills outside the text and hoping that students will apply that instruction to the text in front of them may not have the desired effect because students do not know when or how to apply the particular skill. The skills and standards that a student needs to make one text comprehensible may not be the same ones needed for the next text. Teaching students how to comprehend the text in front of them while scaffolding students through the text's unique challenges results in authentic learning which will support comprehension. If we provide students experience with a preponderance of texts, they will have multiple opportunities to determine which skills they need to apply to comprehend a specific text. An important part of the comprehension discussion is teaching students to determine which skills and strategies will be helpful with each new text they encounter.

Learning to read and comprehending text is not a linear process. We do not learn one skill and then move on. The process is cyclical, and as our texts increase in complexity, so do the demands of our standards. For example, the structure of a primary text is generally not complex; it is often written in a time sequence, but the structure of a secondary text might include flashbacks, foreshadowing, and or parallel storylines. The skills students need to apply depend upon the text they are reading. Standards should not be taught in isolation because multiple standards are needed to make a text comprehensible.

Some skills are inherent to students who have experience with texts and are proficient readers. For example, we don't really need to teach older students to connect prior knowledge to new information or to make personal connections. If a fluent reader is not comprehending, they might not be making connections in their heads, but we don't necessarily have to teach them how to do that. We do need to teach them to be aware that they are not comprehending the text and help them determine why. Content teachers work to help students understand the material of their content, but it is also important for them to help students regulate their reading while offering students a variety of strategies to help them comprehend their content (Snow, 2002).

Although skills and standards need to be explicitly taught, they need to be taught in conjunction with the text without losing sight of the purpose for reading which is comprehension of the entire text.

INSTRUCTIONAL SHIFTS

The implementation of more rigorous state standards has resulted in three major instructional shifts. Student Achievement Partners (2014) has identified the first shift as "building knowledge through content-rich nonfiction and informational text" (para. 1). This is evident in the K–5 classroom with the recommendation being that approximately 50 percent of the text should be informational material which students use to learn about science, social studies, literature, and the arts through the reading process. In the six to twelve classroom, the emphasis on informational text increases to about 70 percent of the reading. Teachers use the text as a vehicle for students to extract, synthesize, and apply content information. Students should grapple with the text to gain the content information, rather than having teachers provide the information from the text orally or in other formats. Consequently, the text itself becomes the source for content learning. The teacher's role shifts from providing the content information to scaffolding the comprehension of textual information.

The second major instructional shift that has occurred as a result of changes in standards is an emphasis on creating "reading and writing grounded in evidence from the text" (Student Achievement Partners, 2014, para. 2). Textual evidence has become an important part of discussions about the text and is necessary for the transition from reading to writing. The goal of instruction is to have students develop text-based answers rather than simply forming text-to-self connections. As a consequence of this instructional shift, students are expected to be able to develop written responses to ideas, events, facts, or an author's point of view. The more rigorous standards have moved instruction away from students simply being asked to write personal responses to text. When responding to a text, informational and argumentative writing should include evidence from the text.

The third shift that Student Achievement Partners (2014) identified was the emphasis on "regular practice with complex text and its academic vocabulary" (para. 3). Teachers need to encourage close and careful reading of increasingly more complex materials. Instruction focuses on grade-appropriate texts and beyond, with scaffolding provided when needed. During this process, academic vocabulary is built through exposure to these more complex texts (NYSDE, n.d.).

CLOSE READING

So, what is close reading? Shanahan (2012) provided a definition of the term. He indicated that close reading is "an intensive analysis of a text in order to come to terms with what it says, how it says it, and what it means" (para. 4). Close reading is a process used for analyzing complex texts that requires a reader to develop a deeper understanding of the content, rather than just determining the main idea or retelling the plot. For some texts, a single first read is all that is necessary because the text does not need to be analyzed on a deeper level. For other texts, a close read would be beneficial, but not every text deserves a close read. Teachers need to choose carefully those texts that would be appropriate for close reading.

When implementing close reading in the classroom, it typically involves multiple readings of the same text. The process usually requires students to focus on a short passage or a smaller portion of a longer passage. Close reading generally involves reading with a pencil, which includes marking the text by underlining, circling, writing in the margins, and annotating the text. Teachers should give students a chance to struggle a bit with the text as they analyze and draw meaning from it for themselves.

One method for close reading is to align your purposes for reading and rereading the text with the clusters of the Common Core standards we discussed previously: the main idea and details of the text, the craft and structure the author used within the text, and the integration of knowledge and ideas within and among texts (Common Core State Standards Initiative, 2014b). These three clusters encompass the ten anchor standards that are used to describe the skills that students need to master for success within the reading process.

Using this method, the first encounter with the text in a close reading focuses on the first cluster, developing an understanding of the key ideas and details. This addresses the first three English Language Arts Common Core anchor standards for reading. Standard 1 discusses determining explicitly stated meanings and making logical inferences. Standard 2 includes determining the main idea and supporting details. Standard 3 examines the interaction of these main ideas and details throughout the text. These three standards, taken together, support the identification of main ideas and details. Before the first reading of the text, the teacher might ask the students to think about what the author of text wants them to understand. On the second read the students might be asked the following question: "What events the author included to show the reader the importance of . . . ?"

However, a close reading of a text requires the student to move past this initial level. The student needs to read the text or a portion of the text a second time, focusing on how the author chose to arrange and present the information, not just the information itself. This second reading would consider the author's organization, word choice, and literary devices used to support the author's development of the topic. These align with the craft and structure cluster of the Common Core standards. This grouping encompasses the next three reading anchor standards. Anchor standard 4 examines the words and phrases the author chose to incorporate. Standard 5 focuses on the structure of the text and the relationships between the sentences, paragraphs, and larger sections. The final standard in this section, standard 6, asks the student to analyze the point of view or purpose of the text. A text-dependent question for this cluster might be: "How does the author's choice of words illustrate the author's point of view about the topic?"

The third reading of the text helps the student to develop an even deeper understanding and focuses on the third cluster, "integration of knowledge and ideas within and between diverse texts and formats." This section again encompasses three anchor standards. Anchor standard 7 addresses the integration of the content in various formats. Standard 8 requires students to evaluate the validity of the author's reasoning. Standard 9 asks the student to compare texts and approaches (Common Core State Standards Initiative, 2014a). A text-dependent task for the final reading might be: "Describe the connection between the first paragraph and the last paragraph of this text."

Although there are many different formats that close reading can follow, it typically involves multiple readings of the text, with each reading having a different focus. There is neither time nor reason for conducting a close reading of every text. For close reading, texts should be chosen based on their complexity. The final standard, anchor standard 10, asserts the ultimate goal of reading instruction—that students should be able to read and comprehend complex texts independently and proficiently (Common Core State Standards Initiative, 2014a).

IMPACT ON COMPREHENSION

In an attempt to determine the factors that impacted students' comprehension, the ACT (2006) analyzed the data from 1.2 million high school students who had taken the ACT and indicated that they would graduate from high school in 2005. The study analyzed students' performance on five types of questions: main idea, supporting details, relationships, meaning of words, and generalizations and conclusions. They found that student performance was at a consistent level across the different types of questions. For example, if students answered 20 percent of the total questions correctly, they tended to answer 20 percent of each different type of question correctly. Students tended to perform at the same level no matter what type of question was asked. This finding was consistent no matter what percentage of questions students answered correctly. So, teaching students additional strategies for answering a specific type of question, would not significantly increase students' scores.

Then instead of analyzing the questions, the ACT researchers analyzed the passages. Interestingly, when the performance was analyzed by the degree of text complexity of the passage, important factors became evident. The researchers found that the more complex the text, the lower the percentage of accuracy no matter which type of question was asked. They determined that there was an average of a 30 percentage point difference between students' scores on the uncomplicated passages and their scores on the complex passages. The complexity of the passage was the factor that had the greatest impact on students' scores. What conclusions can we draw from this? Students need practice with and strategies for comprehending complex text.

IDENTIFYING APPROPRIATE TEXTS

Many classrooms are transitioning from using textbooks and reading series to the use of more primary documents. Consequently, teachers are faced with the problem of identifying appropriately complex texts to prepare their students to comprehend more rigorous texts. It would be wonderful if there were an exact science or method for calculating text complexity, but there is not. Evaluating texts requires the ability to evaluate the combination of quantitative, qualitative, and reader and task features that is appropriate for your students.

Quantitative Factors

The quantitative features of a text are probably the easiest factors to determine. These features can be calculated using various readability formulas. There are many different methods for calculating readability. These methods include the Flesch–Kincaid, Dale–Chall, Fry, SMOG, and Lexiles, just to name a few. Although these are all readability formulas, they don't all necessarily place a given text at the same level. The "Gettysburg Address" illustrates this variety of levels well. The Fry Readability formula places this text at a tenth-grade level. The Dale–Chall readability places it in a seventh- to eighth-grade range. The Flesch–Kincaid places it at an eleventh-grade level. And the SMOG index places it at an eighth-grade level. So this one text could be judged to be appropriate for use anywhere between a seventh- and an eleventh-grade level based upon the readability formula chosen.

Readability formulas calculate the readability level based on such factors as the sentence length, the number of syllables in the word, and the word frequency. However, each of the formulas places a different weight on each of the components. The quantitative features of a text are generally the easiest to determine because they can be calculated using a computer and/or a free online website. Sometimes, the readability level is published and available online or on the back of the book. Because of the variability between the methods, it is helpful to know which readability formula was used to calculate the readability so that you are using the same measure to compare the levels between or among texts.

Lexiles are another method that can be used to help match readers with texts. Lexile scores can range from BR (beginning reader) to 2000. With the advent of the Common Core, the readability ranges for each Lexile band have been updated based upon these more rigorous expectations. Hiebert (2012a) compares the old Lexile ranges with the new Lexile range expectations based upon the revised standards. Teachers' use of Lexiles typically begins with the second- to third-grade band. The old second- to third-grade band was 450–725, and this has been changed to 450–790. The fourth- to fifth-grade band had been 645–845 and was changed to 770–980. The sixth- through eighth-grade band had been 860–1,010 and was revised to 955–1,155. The ninth- and tenth-grade band had been 960–1,115 and was updated to 1,080–1,305. Although all of the grade bands changed, the greatest difference is evident in the eleventh- to twelfth-grade band which now begins at the level where it used to end. The old band had been 1,070–1,220, while the new band is 1,215–1,355 (Hiebert, 2012b).

Qualitative Factors

The qualitative features of a text tend to be more subjective. These features would include the structure of the text, the language conventions and clarity, the knowledge demands, and the levels of meaning. The Common Core State Standards Initiative developed a tool that can be used to more easily determine where the teacher needs to provide additional support with a specific text. Using this tool, you can evaluate the qualitative features of the text. The tool includes a continuum for each of four categories. The teacher places an x on the band continuum for the level of difficulty for each of the four qualitative categories. The further to the right on the continuum the x is placed, the more support your learners will need to be able to successfully handle the passage. The Common Core State Standards Initiatives' graphic tool is located in Table 7.1.

Table 7.1 Qualitative Dimensions of Text Complexity

Category	Notes and Comments on Text; Support for Placement in This Band	Where to Place within the Band?				
		Beginning of Lower Grade	End of Lower Grade	Beginning of Higher Grade	End of Higher Grade	NOT Suited to Band
Structure (both story structure and form of piece)		◆——————————————————————————▶				
Language clarity and conventions (including vocabulary load)		◆——————————————————————————▶				
Knowledge demands (life, content, cultural/literary)		◆——————————————————————————▶				
Levels of meaning and purpose		◆——————————————————————————▶				
Overall placement	Justification	◆——————————————————————————▶				

Common Core State Standards Initiative. (2014). Supplemental Information for Appendix A of the Common Core State Standards for English Language Arts and Literacy: New Research on Text Complexity. Retrieved from http://www.corestandards.org/assets/E0813_Appendix_A_New_Research_on_Text_Complexity.pdf.

Smarter Balance (2011) has also published a gradient for text complexity that might be helpful in identifying the various levels of the features within the text and for determining where your students might need support when working with a particular passage.

Reader and Text

The final category, the reader and text, would be such factors as the student's motivation, prior knowledge, background concepts, and experiences. This category is where the home environment, cultural background, language development, and life exposure all play significant roles.

This issue becomes particularly evident when working with English language learners (ELLs). If ELLs are literate in their own language, then they typically are able to apply the skills of learning to read to their second language. The "universal" or "central processing" framework indicates that both the cognitive and linguistic skills of the first language influence the development of literacy skills in the second language (Geva, 2006).

Much like the advantages of knowledge about a topic when reading a text for a student whose first language is English, ELLs have experiences and knowledge that they bring to a text. What they lack is the ability to convey this knowledge in English. Teachers need to develop ways to help their ELLs connect the knowledge they have to the new information they are learning by incorporating the ELL's culture into the curriculum (Holmes, Rutledge, & Gauthier, 2009). When planning for instruction, teachers need to look for connections between the ELL's culture and the text.

Text-based vocabulary instruction is essential for an ELL's comprehension. Teachers should select the academic vocabulary ELLs would need to know to comprehend the core concepts of the text. Before the text is read, they should introduce the vocabulary. Further support can be provided through the creation of sentence frames for the target vocabulary. A sentence frame is a sentence structured with blanks where students add the missing words. Students might need the additional support of word banks for the sentence frames (Donnelly & Roe, 2010).

There is an abundance of strategies that a teacher can employ to support an ELLs comprehension i.e. key-learning handouts, illustrations, role playing, KWLs, word webs, but the key is to learn about your ELLs' cultures and explore their experiences to help them make connections to the new learning.

Teachers often have a litany of strategies for teaching reading to ELLs and native language speakers but express frustration when these strategies do not produce a classroom of students who are motivated to read. We know that there are two types of motivators, intrinsic and extrinsic. Extrinsic motivators are rewards or grades. Extrinsic motivation comes from outside the student, and it is reasonable to assume that once the extrinsic motivator is removed the behavior will not continue. Intrinsic motivation comes from an internal desire of the student. It might be reading for enjoyment or knowledge about a topic. It is not easy to foster intrinsic motivation for reading, but if a teacher can hook a student on reading by exposing that student to texts of interest, it could lead to interests in additional, connected topics.

Researchers have identified several factors that impact motivation, but the one reoccurring, most often cited factor is choice of reading material. In our already very full academic days, finding time for students to read for enjoyment or to read texts of personal interest seems like a lofty goal. However, if our ultimate goal is to create lifelong readers, we need to provide independent time for choice reading. Students' interest in reading for fun diminishes when what they read is overly controlled by the teacher. Guiding students to connect reading with enjoyment means providing them some choice in what they read (Bennett, 2017).

Feature Overlap

Although text complexity factors can be viewed in isolation, as they seem to be in the text complexity triangle, there is also some overlap between the factors. It might be easier to visualize the overlap using a Venn diagram (see figure 7.1). For example, vocabulary might be quantitative if you are examining the number of syllables in the word. It could be a qualitative factor if you are referring

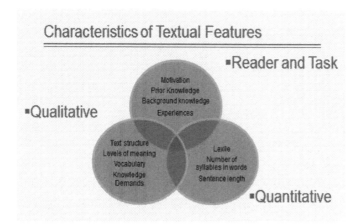

Figure 7.1   Characteristics of Textual Features.

to a dialect, or it could be more related to the reader and the text if you are considering the experiences students have with that particular vocabulary word.

SCAFFOLDING COMPREHENSION

QARs

All teachers, whether they are literacy instructors or content area teachers, will need to guide students' reading. The process of developing questions is an important one. The questions that you use can lead students either back to examining the text more extensively or away from the text to their own ideas and experiences. Oftentimes, question–answer relationships (QARs) have been recommended for helping students comprehend text. These were originally developed based on the research of Raphael and Au (2005) and emphasized the importance of using both text and background information to make sense of the passage. QARs are built on three comprehension strategies: locating information, determining the structure of the text, and determining when an inference is needed. QARs divide questions into two broad types based on where the answer is found: In My Head or In the Book. There are two types of In My Head questions: On My Own, and Author and Me. There are also two types of In the Book questions: Right There, and Think and Search.

The On My Own questions are typically used before reading the text. Their purpose is to attempt to determine the information the reader already has about the topic. The reader typically does not actually have to read the text to answer an On My Own question. During reading, a combination of Right There and Think and Search questions can help to form a balance between text-based, literal questions and inferential questions. After reading, Author and Me questions would be particularly effective in helping students process and apply information and move their understanding toward the deeper critical thinking level (The Reading Lady, n.d.).

Text-Dependent Questions

Using text-dependent questions might be an even more effective instructional practice than QARs. Text-dependent questions move away from QARs' On My Own questions and instead focus on questions that can be answered only by referring back to the text. Text-dependent questions should not require specific background information from the student but instead ask the student to gather, analyze, and synthesize the information presented in the text. Effective text-dependent questions analyze sentences, phrases, or words; examine arguments; note patterns; and consider what is not said within the text (Achieve the Core, 2013).

LITERACY PRACTICES

Especially for literacy instructors, the practices used during your literacy instruction are just as important as the types of questions you incorporate in your lessons. Because of the increased emphasis in using informational texts and primary sources, content area teachers might find many of these practices extremely useful as well. Balanced literacy instruction should provide opportunities for read alouds, shared reading, guided reading, independent reading, word study, and writing.

Read Alouds

The read aloud time is when the teacher reads a book, poem, article, or a short section of a text to the class. This practice helps to develop book, print, and phonological awareness; models accurate reading and fluency; develops listening and reading comprehension skills; and supports vocabulary growth. The teacher will want to carefully choose a text that supplements and builds on other lessons. It is important for teachers to decide ahead of time where to stop and think aloud, and how to provide opportunities for students' responses. A read aloud should be more than just a model of fluent reading. Typically, the read aloud text should be above the students' independent reading level, exposing them to more complex ideas, sentence structures, and vocabulary. However, remember to include opportunities for students to discuss the information presented in the text. This strategy can be used effectively no matter what level of learners you are working with, whether they are kindergarten students or high school seniors.

Shared Reading

Shared reading has many of the same purposes as the read aloud, but during this activity the students are visually following the printed text. Students may read chorally or follow along as the teacher is reading the text orally. This practice builds book, print, and phonics skills; increases reading accuracy and fluency; and helps develop reading comprehension strategies. The shared text should be chosen carefully so that opportunities for repeated reading are incorporated. Shared reading is used most frequently with younger readers. However, Readers Theater is an activity that can be used with older learners in any content area and can be a particularly engaging example of this type of instructional practice.

Guided Reading

Guided reading provides students with the opportunity to practice using decoding and comprehension strategies with a text that is at their instructional level. This practice involves greater student ownership of the text, helps to expand print and book awareness, and develops phonics skills while improving accuracy, fluency, and comprehension. Since guided reading typically occurs in a small groups of elementary learners, this activity allows the teacher to provide more individualized instruction.

Word Study

During word study, the teacher provides direct, systematic instruction in encoding and decoding of words. Its purpose is to help develop phonological awareness, phonics, and vocabulary skills along with students' word and structural analysis skills with single-syllable and multisyllabic words. Word study is an approach that can be used in any grade level or content area. It is a particularly effective practice when introducing new vocabulary in any content area kindergarten through high school.

Writing

In the writing portion of literacy instruction, teachers attempt to move students from teacher-directed to student directed-writing skills and strategies. Writing activities help to increase print, phonics, and vocabulary skills while developing writing skills and strategies in expressing both the content and the mechanics of the writing process (Teaching as Leadership, 2011). Literacy instruction that includes writing is particularly effective for upper elementary through secondary students.

As you are structuring students' interaction with the text, whether you are a literacy teacher or a content area teacher, you will want to provide these different types of opportunities before, during, and after reading so that students can interact and reflect on the content of what they are reading. The following are some activities you might want to consider to meet the needs of your students because they encourage peer discussion and reflection of the content from a complex text to meet the needs of your students.

BEFORE, DURING, AND AFTER READING

Have you ever begun reading a passage and several paragraphs into it found that you had to back up to determine exactly what you were reading about? If we do not activate our thinking prior to reading a text, this is exactly what can happen. Teaching students strategies for before, during, and after reading will help prepare them for the passage and assist in their comprehension of the text.

Before Reading

Before reading, good readers set a specific purpose to help them understand the information they expect to gain from reading the text. As teachers, we should encourage students to preview a passage and predict or generate questions about the text. This prepares the students' brains to make sense of what they are about to read.

Previewing a text could also involve looking at the text features. Nonfiction features might include captions, graphics, illustrations and photographs, labels, maps, and subtitles. These features also include the formatting of the font to include bold, italicized, or underlined text. Fiction text features are not as numerous; however, they could include chapters, photographs and/or pictures, maps, or captions.

Activating background knowledge is an additional method that teachers use for preparing students to read. As teachers, however, we need to take care that we are not providing so much background knowledge that we are depriving students of the opportunity to learn from reading the actual text. Activating background knowledge should be brief and limited to helping students set a purpose for reading.

As teachers, we should also consider providing support for difficult vocabulary prior to students' reading the text. Students should be taught to recognize when unfamiliar vocabulary interferes with comprehension. Strategies for making sense of unknown words include using context clues; looking words up in a glossary or dictionary; analyzing the structural composition of the word based on an understanding of root words, prefixes, and suffixes; or even asking another person for a definition.

Prereading strategies may include brainstorming, skimming and scanning for information, formulating questions prior to reading, or quickly writing for two to five minutes in response to a given question about the topic. Brainstorming could involve writing down individually or in a group, everything the reader knows about the topic. If, prior to reading a text, the readers skim and scan the passage, it helps them prepare for what they are about to read and activates their thinking about the topic. This can also lead to making predictions or generating questions about the upcoming reading. Teachers can also consider posing a question to which students respond in a quick write prior to reading a text.

During Reading

Reading is an active process. During reading, students should be taught to monitor their own comprehension. If comprehension breaks down, students need strategies to repair their lack of understanding. Readers may choose to go back to where confusion began and carefully reread, or they may find that they need to clarify some of the vocabulary with which they are unfamiliar. Often students may find it helpful to stop and briefly summarize small chunks of difficult or lengthy passages.

Understanding the structure of a text can also aid students' comprehension of the passage. Many graphic organizers are available to assist your students in visualizing or breaking down the structure of a text. Plot structure maps, which typically incorporate exposition, rising action, climax, falling action, and resolution, are often used with fiction texts. Nonfiction text structure maps may be organized to focus on sequence or time order, comparison/contrast, problem/solution, cause/effect, and description or listing. In reading nonfiction, if students understand the structure of the text, it can often help them to determine the author's purpose.

Text coding, annotating, or marking a text with questions or thoughts can assist students in comprehension of the passage. Stopping at various intervals to discuss a text is also an effective during-reading strategy that can help make a text comprehensible. Additionally, making personal connections to the text and connecting the text to other texts and the world (Keene & Zimmerman, 1997) can assist and expand students' understanding.

During reading, strategies may include monitoring and adjusting reading rate, chunking the text, or visualizing. As students are reading a complex text, they may find that they need to adjust their reading rate. They may need to slow down for portions of a text that are more challenging than others, and, conversely, they may find that they can quickly read through portions of a text with which they have some familiarity. If a text is lengthy or difficult to understand, students can chunk the text by breaking it into shorter portions to assist in comprehension. Stopping at each chunked section to think about or write about that portion of the text can enhance the overall understanding of the text. To assist students in visualizing the content, you may choose to have readers stop and illustrate the text, or have them search for visual examples of the text on the Internet. Both of these activities may assist students in expanding their understanding.

After Reading

Summarizing, paraphrasing, reviewing, or spending time interpreting a text after reading will enhance comprehension and retention of information from the passage. After reading, it may be helpful to have students revisit some of their before reading activities. Students can adjust the predictions they made prior to reading, or they can identify the questions that still remain after reading the topic. Another effective way to summarize might be to have students add to information that was brainstormed prior to reading. In addition, reflecting in writing about what they have read is a strategy that will support comprehension and provide the teacher a window into students' understanding of a passage.

ASSESSMENT

Reading comprehension is a multifaceted skill that all students need. Students must be able to recognize written words, understand the meaning of words and sentences, relate their prior knowledge to what they are reading, synthesize information, make inferences and predictions, draw conclusions, and analyze texts and passages. These activities need to all occur simultaneously.

Formal Assessments

Formal assessments tend to be the standardized assessments that generate data about how a student is doing in comparison to a standard or a reference group. These assessments could be norm referenced, which compare a student's performance to his grade-level peers, or criterion referenced, which provide information about how the student's performance compares to a specific standard. The data from these types of assessments are mathematically calculated to evaluate student performance. Group-administered state or district assessments, as well as individually administered assessments such as the Developmental Reading Assessment, the Gray Oral Reading Test, the Woodcock Reading Mastery Tests, the Iowa Test of Basic Skills, and basal series reading assessments, are all examples of formal assessments.

Typically these assessments include a passage the student reads, followed by questions to be answered. Depending on the assessment, these assessments might be timed or untimed, but the questions generally cover understanding the main idea and details, making predictions, drawing conclusions, determining the author's purpose and mood, evaluating the validity of the arguments, and establishing relationships within, between, and among texts.

Informal Assessments

Informal assessments tend to be more content than data driven. The purpose of an informal assessment is to ensure that, as students are reading, they comprehend the material. Running records are informal assessments because, instead of generating numerical percentiles or standard scores, they generate such information as reading rate measured in words correct per minute, miscues, and/or the number of questions answered correctly. This information is used to inform instruction rather than to compare the student to other students or a standard. The Informal Reading Inventory, the Qualitative Reading Inventory, rubrics, and cloze procedures would be additional examples of informal assessments.

Progress Monitoring

Within the classroom, teachers also use ongoing methods of progress monitoring to determine if students are processing the textual information as they read. These would include such activities as answers to teacher-prepared questions, written journal responses, projects, and portfolios. Writing is an excellent vehicle for assessing students' understanding. Students' written responses, portfolios, and projects can be used to demonstrate the depth of their understanding of a topic. These projects would be examples of authentic alternative assessments. An authentic assessment mirrors the reading and writing activities that occur in the real world. Portfolio assessments, ongoing collections of student work, are a particularly effective way to document growth over time.

COMPREHENSION ASSESSMENTS FOR CLASSROOM USE

Oral Retellings

Oral retellings are a strategy that can be used with both narrative and expository texts, and are an effective way to determine if students understand the passage (Stahl, 2009). An oral retelling can be used with a brief text that has been read orally or silently. The passage should be limited to about 500 words or less, depending on the age of the student. Ask the students to retell the information as though they were telling it to someone who has never heard the text before. For ease in scoring, it may be helpful for the teacher to have a list of the main ideas and details from the text that way the information can just be checked off rather than having to write out the student's responses. For narrative texts, students should include the setting, characters, major events, resolution, and sequence. For expository or informational texts, students should include the main ideas and supporting details from each section. With frequently used passages, teachers might find it helpful to create a scoring guide that lists the major points with the total number of possible points for the passage so that a tally mark can be recorded for each response. The totals from the scoring guide can be used to generate the percentage of the details included in the retelling.

Content-Area Reading Inventory

The Content-Area Reading Inventory (Readence et al., 1992) is a three-part assessment. To administer the assessment, teachers need a text selection from a textbook and a teacher-created reading inventory for the text. The first part of the inventory should consist of four to six questions about the features within the text such as the index, glossary, captions, headings, introductions, and summaries. The second section should contain four to six questions related to Tiers Two and Three vocabulary knowledge, figurative language, and context clues. The final section, which is the most important, should contain seven to nine questions related to literal, inferential, and critical comprehension of the text, and its organization, structure, and integration of ideas.

Readence et al. (1992) recommended that for easy reading, students should answer 86–100 percent of the questions correctly. Materials where students earn between 64 and 85 percent of the questions correct would be appropriate for use with teacher support. If the student scores below 64 percent, the material may be too difficult for this particular student.

COMPREHENSION ACTIVITIES

Cubes

On each side of a six-sided dice, the teacher writes one of the following words: who, what, when, where, why, how. To individualize this activity for a specific passage, one or more of these single-word questions could be changed to a question specifically related to the content of the text. Divide the class into small groups. The group of students stands around a table or desk. One student in the group rolls the cube. When the cube stops rolling, the student closest to the cube must answer the question on the side of the cube that is facing up.

Indirect Characterization

This activity is appropriate for use with fictional texts. Divide your class into groups of five students. Write the names of characters from the fiction text your class is reading on small slips of paper. Put the names in a container, and have one person from each group of five students draw a name. Assign to each member of the group a different one of the five indirect characterization techniques from the list that follows. Instruct students to use their texts to help them create clues that reveal the personality of their character based on these methods for indirect characterization.

1. *Speech*: What does the character say? How does the character speak?
2. *Private thoughts*: What does the character think?
3. *Actions*: What actions reveal the character's personality?
4. *Physical appearance*: What does the character look like? How does this character dress? How or where does he or she live?
5. *Effect on others*: How do others view the character?

Each group member describes the character to the class based upon a trait that was assigned to them: speech, private thoughts, actions, physical appearance, or effect on others. This can be done in the first or third person. As an extension, the group can create a visual representation of their character based upon what they learned about the character.

Give One—Get One

After the class has read the informational or narrative text, the teacher poses a question or states a topic related to the reading. Students number their papers from 1 to 5. For items numbered 1, 2, and 3, students must independently write a possible answer to the question or facts about the stated topic. Students then pair with another student. They each share one of their answers, and if it is a new answer, they add it as the fourth item on their list. Students keep changing partners until they have added the fifth possible answers or facts. They may also use these discussions as an opportunity to correct any of their original responses if they discover an error in their thinking.

Inference Venn Diagrams

Inferences are formed when combining background knowledge with information from a text. This activity helps to scaffold students as they are creating inferences based on textual information. Students create a Venn diagram by drawing two intersecting circles on a sheet of paper, creating an overlapping section large enough to record information. Students write their background information about the topic in the left-hand circle. In the right-hand circle, students write information from the text. In the overlapping sections, students write inferences by combining their background information with information from the text.

Word Splash

A word splash is a collection of words, phrases, or concepts from the text that students are about to read or have just read. The terms are "splashed" on a page for students to see. Word splashes can be either teacher or student created. If the teacher creates the word splash to use before reading the text, students use as many words as possible to write predictions about the text prior to reading it; after reading the passage, they correct the statements based on what was learned from the text.

Student-created word splashes can be used after reading the text. The group of students decides on the most important words related to the topic and arranges these as a word splash. They can then give the word splash to a different group of students so that they can create summarizing sentences based on the words in the word splash. Word splashes can also be created using digital programs.

RAFT

This writing strategy is used to summarize the information from a passage and to present it from a specific viewpoint. The process can be used easily to represent opposing views in a story, conflicting sides in a historic event, or an object involved in a scientific process. RAFT is an acronym that explains the components of the written assignment. R refers to the role, A the audience for whom the piece is written, F the form or format of the writing, and T the specific topic based on the text. The role is the perspective from which the piece is written. The text is written from the first-person perspective as though the writer is that object or person indicated in the role. Students will need to consider who would be interested in reading this information. That would be the audience for whom the piece is written. The format could be an essay, a letter, a memo, a list, a postcard, a poem, or the like, depending on how much information you want the students to include. The topic would be the topic of the original piece the students read. A few examples could include a prisoner of war, a number in a mathematical process, characters in a novel, and an object in a chemical reaction (Santa et al., 1988).

Shape Up Review

This activity can be used to summarize the information in a passage. A sheet of paper is divided into thirds horizontally. In the top third, students draw a large box. In each corner of the box, students record one idea from the text that "squares" with their thinking.

In the center section of the paper, students draw a large triangle. In each vertex of the triangle, students write a vocabulary term that describes an important feature of the topic.

In the bottom section of the sheet of paper, students draw a large circle. In the circle, students write a summary statement that encompasses the main idea of the passage.

ABC Organizer

This strategy is most often used during reading or to summarize a topic. Students create a chart with twenty-six boxes. At the top of each box, they write one letter of the alphabet. This activity can be simplified to include only nine or twelve boxes by placing multiple letters of the alphabet in a single box. Students may work individually or in groups; however, groups would allow for more extensive discussion about the topic and would help to scaffold those students who need additional support.

During or after reading the text, students place in each box one word that begins with the letter or letters at the top of the box. The objective is to fill each box with at least one word. As an extension, students can determine which words are most significant and organize these words into larger categories to summarize the topic more fully.

Semantic Feature Analysis

This graphic organizer strategy is especially effective for comparing the components of a larger topic. The graphic organizer can be created before reading the text to help the students identify what information to focus on during reading, or it can be used after reading as a review of the concepts. For example, if the topic were seasons, the components of the topic would be fall, winter, spring, and summer. These components of the major topic would be written on horizontal rows in the far left-hand column of the semantic feature analysis chart.

Characteristics that might or might not describe each of the subtopics are written as the caption for the vertical columns of the chart. The horizontal rows and vertical columns form a grid. If a subtopic has that feature, students place an *x* in the box under the characteristic. If it does not, the students leave that block blank. If the students are not sure, they can place a question mark in the box and then after reading go back and complete the information (Johnson & Pearson, 1978).

Concept Map

This activity works well as a prereading activity. The concept map can then be refined throughout the unit of study. Before reading the text, a key word or topic is identified by the teacher and placed in the center of the board, paper, or projection. As students suggest other terms or ideas that are related to the identified central topic, the terms can be arranged as isolates or in clusters.

After reading the text, students suggest additional terms that demonstrate their expanded understanding of the topic. These are written in a different color and placed within the appropriate clusters. This strategy helps students to visualize the relationships between the topics and organize the information from the text. It also visually distinguishes prior knowledge from newly acquired information.

REFERENCES

Achieve the Core. (2013). Guide to creating text-dependent questions. Retrieved from http://achievethecore.org/page/46/complete-guide-to-creating-text-dependent-questions-detail-pg.

ACT. (2006). *Reading between the Lines: What the ACT Reveals about College Readiness in Reading.* Retrieved from http://www.act.org/research/policymakers/pdf/reading_report.pdf.

Alberti, S. (2013). Making the shifts. *Educational Leadership, 70*(4), 24–27. Retrieved from http://www.ascd.org/publications/educational-leadership/dec12/vol70/num04/Making-the-Shifts.aspx.

Australian United States Services in Education (AUSSIE). (n.d.). *A Beginner's Guide to Text Complexity.* NYCDOE Secondary Literacy Project. Retrieved from http://schools.nyc.gov/NR/rdonlyres/A6EB078F-25AF-4AC1-8C2E-B16CC28BD4 7F/0/Beginnersguidetotextcomplexity_FINAL_72811.docx.

Bennett, C. (2017, March 30). Reading choice encourages student ownership. *ThoughtCo.* Retrieved from http://thoughtco.com/reading-choice-and-motivation -4135606.

Calkins, L., Ehrenworth, M., & Lehman, C. (2012). *Pathways to the Common Core: Accelerating Achievement.* Portsmouth, NH: Heinemann.

Carlisle, J. F. & Rice, M. S. (2002). *Improving Reading Comprehension: Research-Based Principles and Practices.* Baltimore: York Press.

Carmen, P. (2009). *Skeleton Creek.* Jefferson City, MO: Scholastic.

Cole, J. (1990). *The Magic School bus Lost in Space.* Jefferson City, MO: Scholastic.

Common Core State Standards for English Language Arts & Literacy in History/Social Studies, Science, and Technical Subjects. (2010). *Appendix A: Research Supporting Key Elements of the Standards.* Retrieved from http://www.corestandards.org/assets/Appendix_A.pdf.

Common Core State Standards Initiative. (2014a). *English Language Arts Standards: Anchor Standards: College and Career Readiness Anchor Standards for Reading.* Retrieved from http://www.corestandards.org/ELA-Literacy/CCRA/R/.

Common Core State Standards Initiative. (2014b). *Supplemental Information for Appendix A of the Common Core State Standards for English Language Arts and Literacy: New Research on Text Complexity.* Retrieved from http://www.corestandards.org/assets/E0813_Appendix_A_New_Research_on_Text_Complexity.pdf.

Donnelly, W. B., & Roe, C. J. (2010). Using sentence frames to develop academic vocabulary for English learners. *The Reading Teacher, 64*(2), 131–136.

Doty, J. K., Cameron, G. N., & Barton, M. L. (2003). *Teaching Reading in Social Studies.* Aurora, CO: Mid-continent Research for Education and Learning.

Frank, A. (1952). *The Diary of a Young Girl.* New York: Doubleday & Company.

Frayer, D. (n.d.). Frayer model. Retrieved from http://wvde.state.wv.us/strategybank/FrayerModel.html.

Gantos, J. (1998). *Joey Pigza Swallowed the Key.* Harrisonburg, VA: R. R. Donnelley & Sons Company.

Garrison, S. (2016, September 23). What are "text sets," and why use them in the classroom? [Blog post]. Retrieved from fordhaminstitute.org/national/commentary/what-are-text-sets-and-why-use-them-classroom.

Geva, E. (2006). *Learning to Read in a Second Language: Research, Implications, and Recommendations for Services.* Centre of Excellence for Early Childhood Development. University of Toronto, Canada.

Glasswall, K., & Ford, M. P. (2010). Teaching flexibility with leveled texts: More power for your reading block. *The Reading Teacher, 64*(1), 57–60.

Harvey, S., & Goudvis, A. (2017). *Strategies that Work: Teaching Comprehension for Understanding, Engagement, and Building Knowledge* (3rd ed.). Markham, ON: Pembroke Publishers.

Hiebert, E. H. (2012a). The Common Core's staircase of text complexity: Getting the size of the first step right. *Reading Today, 29*(3), 26–28. Retrieved from www.r eading.org/Libraries/reading-today-daily/TextComplexity_RTy_Jan2012.pdf.

Hiebert, E. H. (2012b). *The Common Core State Standard of Text Complexity: What Does it Mean? How Can We Make It Happen?* Retrieved from http://textproject. org/assets/library/powerpoints/Hiebert_2011-02-22_Pearson-CCSS-Virtual-Confe rence.pdf.

Holmes, K. P., Rutledge, S. & Gauthier, L. R. (2009, November/December). Understanding the cultural-linguistic divide in American classrooms: language learning strategies for a diverse student population. *Reading Horizons: A Journal of Literacy and Language Arts, 49*(4), 287–289.

Johnson, D. D., & Pearson, P. D. (1978). *Teaching Reading Vocabulary.* New York: Holt, Rinehart, and Winston.

McGraw-Hill. (2005). Reading comprehension and considerate text. Retrieved from http://www.glencoe.com/sec/teachingtoday/subject/considerate_text.phtml.

New York City Department of Education. (n.d.). *Crosswalk of Common Core Instructional Shifts: ELA/Literacy.* Retrieved from http://schools.nyc.gov/NR/rdonlyres /058ED42A-2857-4747-8E41-39BF89BCC374/0/CommonCoreInstructionalSh ifts_ELALiteracy.pdf.

Raphael, T. E., & Au, K. H. (2005). QAR: Enhancing comprehension and test taking across grades and content areas. *The Reading Teacher*, 59, 206–221.

Readence, J. E., Bean, T. W., & Baldwin, R. S. (1992). *Content Area Reading: An Integrated Approach* (4th ed.). Dubuque, IA: Kendall/Hunt.

Recht, D. R., & Leslie, L. (1988). Effect of prior knowledge on good and poor readers' memory of text. *Journal of Educational Psychology, 80*(1), 16–20.

Santa, C. M., Havens, L., Nelson, M., Danner, M., Scalf, L., & Scalf, J. (1988). *Content Reading Including Study Systems: Reading, Writing, and Studying across the Curriculum.* Dubuque, IA: Kendall/Hunt.

Shanahan, T. (2012, June). What is close reading? *Shanahan on Literacy.* Retrieved from http://www.shanahanonliteracy.com/2012/06/what-is-close-reading.html.

Smarter Balance. (2011). Gradients in complexity: Text complexity rubric for informational text. Retrieved from http://literacy.psesd.org/wp-content/uploads/sites /2/2014/02/8-SBAC-Gradients-in-Complexity-Informational-Texts.docx.

Snow, C. (2002). *Reading for Understanding: Toward an R & D Program in Reading Comprehension.* Chicago, IL: Rand. Retrieved from https://www.rand.org/pubs/ monograph_reports/MR1465.html.

Stahl, K. A. D. (2009). Assessing the comprehension of young children. In S. E. Israel & G. G. Duffy (Eds.), *Handbook on Research on Reading Comprehension* (pp. 428–448). New York: Routledge.

Student Achievement Partners. (2014). *Crosswalk of Common Core Instructional Shifts: ELA/Literacy.* Retrieved from http://schools.nyc.gov/NR/rdonlyres/058E D42A-2857-4747-8E41-39BF89BCC374/0/CommonCoreInstructionalShifts_ ELALiteracy.pdf.

Teaching as Leadership. (2011). *Structuring your Literacy Classroom: A Balanced Literacy Block (K–5).* Retrieved from http://teachingasleadership.org/sites/default/ files/Related-Readings/EL_Ch8_2011.pdf.

Tharp, R. G., & Gallimore, R. (1988). *Rousing Minds to Life: Teaching, Learning, and Schooling in Social Context.* New York: Cambridge University Press.

The Reading Lady. (n.d.). *QAR: Question-Answer-Relationship.* Retrieved from http: //www.readinglady.com/mosaic/tools/QARQuestionAnswerRelationshipTeachi ngChildrenWheretoSeekAnswerstoQuestions.pdf.

Vygotsky, L. (1978). Interaction between learning and development. In *Mind and Society* (pp. 79–91). Cambridge, MA: Harvard University Press. Retrieved from http://www.psy.cmu.edu/~siegler/vygotsky78.pdf.

Chapter 8

Writing

CLASSROOM VISIT

Mrs. Smith sat at her desk grading written responses from the morning's comprehension check. Students just completed reading Edgar Allen Poe's "The Telltale Heart," and were to respond to the question, "Is the narrator sane or insane?" While reading, they had completed a graphic organizer categorizing and describing the narrator's feelings, actions, words, and thoughts. They had been allowed to use their organizer for the writing assessment which required evidence from the text with commentary that explained their thinking.

As she graded, she made notes of what the students, generally, did well. They had pretty strong claims and they were able to pick out mostly relevant evidence to support their claims, but they just could not explain their thinking. They could not explain how the evidence they cited supported their claim.

Mrs. Smith did not know what to do next. She had discussed reliable and unreliable narrators. She had modeled the writing process, and she had students examine examples and non-examples of good commentary but none of that seemed to have paid off. This writing was falling short. It was like students were just being compliant; there was little evidence of their independent thinking in their responses.

Mrs. Smith needed a plan. She decided to bring samples of her students' writing to her next Professional Learning Community meeting and ask for help. Hopefully, some of her fellow teachers would have some good samples and even better advice.

LITERARY CONNECTION

Dear Teacher,
   Whenever I had something to tell you,
   I tugged on your shirt and whispered in your ear.
   This time I'm writing a letter.

   I hope you remember me.
   I was the one who marched to school that first day,
   splashing through every puddle I could find.
   I wore a bright yellow raincoat and a dark, stormy frown-
   because for me, school meant sitting still and listening,
   two things I wasn't much good at.

   I stood there ornery and dripping,
   Just sure I'd get in trouble.
   But instead you grinned at me.
   "Good morning! Look at you,
   Standing there like Mary Kingsley
   Just back from canoeing up the Ogooué River."

   "Who?" I said. "Where?"
   "Mary Kingsley, the fearless explorer," you explained.
   "Someday we'll read about her—and crocodiles.
   Now get the mop."
   Crocodiles!

                  A Letter to My Teacher by Hopkinson and Carpenter

USING WRITING TO SUPPORT READING

In the literacy connection from Hopkinson and Carpenter's *Letter to My Teacher*, the author demonstrates the development of her writing skills to express an experience from her youth in an adult manner. She is taking an experience and expressing it in a way she would not have been able to as a child.

   Unlike reading skills which tend to be well-developed by the end of the school experience, developing writing skills is a lifelong process that continues throughout adulthood. In fact, "only one out of four twelfth-grade students is a proficient writer" (Salahu-Din, Persky, & Miller, 2008). Typically, greater emphasis has been placed on learning to read than on learning to write (Russell, 2006). Graham (2006) indicated that teachers across all grade levels were inconsistent in providing writing instruction covering a wide range of writing strategies. Consequently, it is important for each teacher to fully understand what skills students will be expected to use effectively in their writing and how this process can help to increase reading comprehension.

Although the strategies used by teachers varied depending on grade level and teachers' individual preference, Richards and Strum (n.d.) determined through survey data that across the elementary grades, teachers most frequently used literature as a model for teaching writing. Mini-lessons and guided practice would be another frequently used strategy for writing instruction (Gibson, 2008). Harris and Graham (1996) reported that worksheets and other activities that are not embedded within actual writing experiences did not improve students' writing abilities.

Richards and Strum's (n.d.) survey results indicated that the frequency of writing instruction decreased throughout the elementary grades and that teachers expected students to have mastered the foundation of how to write by fifth grade.

"Reading and writing are reciprocal processes; they're both constructive, meaning making processes" (Tompkins, 2017, p. 61). They work together to support the development of literacy abilities and they facilitate the learning of content (Close, Hull, & Langer, 2005). Because of the relationship between reading and writing, students who read substantially will likely write more easily. Effective writers can also become better readers because writing contributes to an understanding of the relationships between letters and sounds which contributes to the writers' phonemic awareness and phonics knowledge. Writing also deepens the students' understanding of word choice and the structure of texts, which can help them make sense of the text when reading (NCTE, 2016). In addition, writing can facilitate thinking about text. If students write about their reading, it can help clarify their understanding of the passage. Students who write about what they are reading demonstrate more evidence of thinking critically about the passage (Biancarosa & Snow, 2006).

PRIMARY WRITING

It should come as no shock that beginning readers are by nature beginning writers. These emerging writers need instruction in the writing process. Simply providing opportunities to write does not generate the knowledge needed to help students improve their writing skills (Englert, 1992). It is evident that listening, speaking, reading, and writing are interrelated skills and that growth in each of these skill areas is supported by growth in the others (Cisco, 2004). These primary learners need effective writing instruction in the mechanics, organization, and fluent expression of their ideas provided through "richly textured opportunities for students' conceptual and linguistic development" (Goldenberg, 1992, p. 317). Through collaboration with students, teachers provide explicit teaching by modeling, prompting, encouraging, and problem solving (Englert, Mariage, & Dunsmore, 2006).

Learning to read and learning to write are both built on the foundation of oral language and an understanding of textual construction in a variety of genre. Clay (1998) reinforces the reciprocal relationship between learning to read and learning to write. Effective reading and writing instruction contain many of the same features: knowing the functions and purposes of reading and writing, phonological and graphemic awareness, and knowledge of writing strategies (Fitzgerald & Shanahan, 2000). Formal writing instruction typically begins in kindergarten and first grade. Interestingly, students receive a majority of their exposure to writing instruction in the primary, rather than secondary classrooms. It is typically in these primary classrooms that students have the most opportunities to engage in composing various genres of increasing complexity (Richards & Strum, n.d.).

Most exemplary writing instructors use a combination of process and skills instruction (Bromley, 2007). Process approaches focus on learning to plan, draft, edit, revise, and publish writing (Englert, 1992), while skills approaches focus on lower-level skills, like handwriting, grammar, spelling, and punctuation (Bromley, 2007). Effective teachers also teach and model all components of the writing process for their students (Bromley, 2007; Graham & Perin, 2007). Modeling and scaffolding are used to teach students various writing strategies and how to successfully use them while writing. However, over time, teachers reduce the level of scaffolding provided until their students can independently use the strategy.

For first-grade students, who are beginning writers, drawing serves as part of the planning phase of writing. In addition to drawing, they should be taught strategies that will support brainstorming and organization of ideas. Repeated opportunities to implement these strategies, with appropriate scaffolds, would support the development of more sophisticated planning skills. Mini-lessons can aid students in learning how to manage mechanics, spelling, and organization during the writing process.

INTERMEDIATE WRITING

As students move into the intermediate grades, teachers often allow writers less choice in self-selected topics which tends to decrease motivation. This expectation of having students complete writing assignments based on teacher-selected topics or prompts tends to increase the difficulty of the writing (Richards & Strum, n.d.) because of more limited background knowledge. Consequently, with more limited knowledge students have difficulty retrieving the content so their writing tends to lack fluency.

As students mature, they are expected to use planning strategies and graphic organizers more extensively. Writers, especially struggling writers, need additional support in mastering methods for idea generation and organization before they begin writing. Mini-lessons are an effective strategy for supporting struggling writers during the planning stage. This format allows for additional explanation and modeling. Students should be taught how to transfer information from the text into the planning organizer and then incorporate that information into their written responses. Strategy tip sheets containing central ideas from the mini-lesson could be used to assist students in applying new concepts independently (Richards & Strum, n.d.). Through this process, graphic organizers can be used as scaffolding devices to organize the students' responses as well as provide for a gradual increase in the amount of writing required (Stowe, 2011).

Based upon Richards and Strum's (n.d.) survey data, journaling was an activity used frequently in third- and fifth-grade classrooms. Hillocks (1986), however, reported that a large number of studies found that journaling activities, which tend to be more narrative, did not result in improvements in academic writing quality. Instead of free-journaling activities, he recommended that teachers should provide students systematic instruction and consistent feedback in a structured format across a variety of genres to improve academic writing.

MIDDLE GRADES WRITING

As students move into the middle grades writing to support reading comprehension becomes even more important. According to *Writing to Read* (Graham & Hebert, 2010), there are four effective ways to have students write about text. All of these strategies were found to be effective; however, the most effective way was to have students respond to a text in writing through personal reactions and analyzing and interpreting the text. The next most effective strategy was to have students summarize the content. This method was followed by having students write notes about the information. The final effective strategy identified, although not as effective as the previous three, was to have students answer or generate questions about the text.

Taking notes during lectures and summarizing readings are higher-order thinking activities that require students to paraphrase expository content and use extensive meta-linguistic and meta-cognitive resources. Each genre and content area requires a student to gather and organize information in a specific way (Richards & Strum, n.d.). Consequently, students need to be taught a variety of writing skills and processes and where and when to apply these. Students need to learn about the text structures for writing paragraphs, sentence construction skills, and spelling skills (Graham & Hebert, 2010). To assist students in composing written assignments using different genres, mini-lessons can be created that focus on the components required in the specific genre. Strategy tip sheets and different genre concept maps can be created for specifically for each assignment.

HIGH SCHOOL WRITING

By the time students get to high school, we would expect them to have had multiple opportunities to practice writing about text through note-taking, summaries, answering questions, reflections, and analysis. They should continue with these practices in their secondary years to help make sense of the ever-increasing, complex texts to which they are exposed. As we indicated earlier, students' comprehension improves when they write about the text. High school students should be encouraged to read complex texts with a pencil in hand to allow for annotations and note-taking.

Preparing students for life beyond high school becomes paramount at the high school level. This will be one of our last opportunities to fill gaps in students' reading and writing competencies. Our goal should be to create effective readers and writers who are prepared to think independently, participate in higher education, contribute to their workplace, and become responsible citizens who are able to read and recognize reliable information in our ever-increasing, information-intensive world (Fisher, Frey, & ElWardi, 2005). Providing students opportunities to write about their reading will help them make sense of complex texts and controversial issues that will impact them as young adults.

Unfortunately, writing about text may benefit proficient writers more than it does writers who struggle, but just as we scaffold struggling readers, we need to scaffold struggling writers (Loewus, 2016). Providing struggling readers with a graphic organizer specific to the text will support comprehension. Providing time for readers to share and compare their writing about the text will help to clarify and adjust their understanding.

Marzano's Record-Compare-Revise-Combine-Review cycle, R-C-R-C-R, is a strategy that can be used to support readers and writers of many levels. The cycle begins with students creating a summary to record their understanding of content. In the second phase, students compare their writing with a peer looking for similarities or differences and clarifying points of confusion. In the third phase, students polish their drafts by revising their original writing to reflect any new understanding. Marzano's cycle continues with combining the R-C-R cycles to create generalizations on the topic and ends with reviewing the summaries of all the content on a topic (Marzano, 2012).

The beauty of writing is that it can take many forms. High school students generally take notes in their content classes; however, taking notes about what is read and learned is only helpful if the notes are processed. Although it's impossible to write without thinking, it *is* possible to copy notes without thinking. If we want our students to think, we need to instruct them on how to take notes that reflect what they are learning.

Focused note-taking is a strategy that supports note-taking as a process. It involves five steps. The first step is *Creating Notes* by selecting, paraphrasing, and arranging information. The second step is *Processing Notes* by highlighting, adding information, or deleting information. This is followed with *Connecting Thinking* by asking questions or identifying points of confusion. The fourth step is *Summarizing and Reflecting on Learning* by crafting a summary of the most important information. In the final step, students are *Applying Learning* by using notes as a resource for assignments or activities. Throughout the note-taking process students compare their notes with partners and make necessary adjustments. Students can discuss one another's questions and wonderings to deepen their thinking about the notes they take (McKinney, Glazebrook, Sanders, & Shapiro, 2018). Focused note-taking helps students organize and deepen their understanding.

Throughout this book we have talked about the importance of building students' knowledge to support comprehension of complex texts. Writer and teacher Kelly Gallagher publishes on his website "Articles of the Week." These current event articles are just one possible way to support close reading of texts that builds knowledge about our world. In these articles, students are asked to mark points of confusion and respond in writing to the texts. Specific questions are provided to scaffold the writing if necessary. Providing high school students authentic purposes for reading and writing in response to current events will help prepare them for life beyond high school. Kelly Gallagher's articles of the week are excellent models of authentic writing in response to reading experiences for high school students (Gallagher, 2019).

WRITING SUPPORTS COMPREHENSION

Graham and Hebert (2010) in their report for the Carnegie Corporation entitled "Writing to Read: Evidence for How Writing Can Improve Reading" found that "extended writing has a strong and consistently positive impact on reading" (p. 14). The extended responses referenced in their report were either personal reactions or analysis and interpretation of the texts. Writing in response to the text had a greater impact on comprehension than just reading it, rereading it, reading and studying or discussing it, or even reading instruction. Writing in response to reading requires that students engage with and critically think about the text. Writing about text forces students to think!

WRITING ACTIVITIES

Beginning Sentence Writing

Beginning writing starts with learning how to construct a sentence, then a paragraph, and then a paper. Many students who lack experience constructing sentences find the writing process difficult. In the beginning of the writing process, pictures, drawn by students or chosen from magazines, can provide a springboard for idea generation. Students can begin by writing or dictating a sentence about the picture they have drawn or chosen.

Example Cards

Many students will benefit from having a model of sentence construction in front of them for reference. The teacher can also use this model as a teaching aid. Teachers can use an index card with an example sentence for easy reference that is placed where students can see it as sentence construction is being taught. An example of a sample card with very simple sentence construction is as follows:

Table 8.1 Sentence Card

Subject (Who or What)	Verb (Action)	Predict (What Is It About)
I	eat	pizza.
Matt	drew	a picture.

These beginning cards are very simple and use action verbs and simple nouns in the predicate. More complex cards can be made as the students progress in their ability to write sentences. These cards can also be used along with other strategies.

Arrange the Words

Students are given several words to arrange in the correct order to make a logical sentence. For example, the students may be given the three words, "I," "ice cream," and "like." This activity can be completed individually or with a partner. The students can either physically arrange the words or one student can indicate which word should be used to start the sentence, and a partner could move the word so that it becomes the first word in the sentence. The students can continue to work together until all the words have been arranged in an order that makes sense. Another version of this activity would be to place numbers over the words. One student selects the number and the partner arranges the words in the desired order.

Complete the Sentence

In this strategy, students are told a short story and are then given incomplete sentences to complete based upon the content of the story. The teacher may begin by sharing a sentence that has a missing subject (e.g., _____ ate a hamburger). The teacher explains what a subject is and suggests possible words that could be used to complete the sentence. After students learn about completing simple subjects, sentences are given with the verb missing (e.g., Tom ____ home). Discussions about verbs then occur and possible verbs are given. Finally, the sentence is given with any combinations of the subject, verb, and/or predicate missing (e.g., Jerome likes _____). Usually simple nouns are first introduced into the predicate. Over time, less and less of the sentence is provided to encourage more independent writing skills (e.g., ___saw a _____). Eventually, the student may be only provided with a topic and can write the sentence independently.

Expand the Sentence Game

Once students are able to produce correct syntax and write simple comprehensible sentences, the complexity of the sentence can be increased. Some students use very few adjectives or adverbs in their sentences. One way to encourage more complex sentences is to first write the student's sentence. Then the teacher provides a card that lists the words: size, shape, kind, color, how many, when, where, how, and how much. The students examine the sentence to see if it can be expanded to include words from any of the indicated categories. The sentence is rewritten as more information is added to it. This activity can be completed as a game in which the students make check marks by the descriptors that they were able to use in the sentence. They receive a point for each word correctly added to the sentence.

Table 8.2 Expanded Sentence Card

	Size	Shape	Kind	Color	How Many	When	Where	How	How Much	Total Points
Sam	x								x	3
Jane		x	x	x	x					4
Phil	x					x				2

Beginning Paragraph Writing

Software is available to assist students with the process of writing paragraphs and papers. Numerous apps are available that can be used to record students' thoughts. These programs can help students with the prewriting and organization of their thought through the use of concept maps or webs. The actual writing of the paragraph or story is supported with outlines based upon the web created.

Story Maps

Story maps are graphic organizers used to provide visual representations about the elements that compose a story such as characters, setting, problem, and resolution. These may be very simple with younger students and can become more complicated as students mature. A simple story map is illustrated below.

Table 8.3 Story Map

Beginning	Middle	End
The story starts when . . .	After that . . .	The story ends with . . .

Story Frames

Story frames focus on the structure of the story and help students to organize the story information. To complete the story frame, students need to provide basic information about the events in the story. This can be done collaboratively. A story frame provides the beginning of the sentence followed by a blank that the students need to fill in. It may look as simple as something like this:

The problem in the story is _____.
The problem is solved when _____.
In the end of the story _____.

Story frames that are more complex can be created for more advanced students.

Directed Reading and Thinking Activity (DRTA)

A Directed Reading and Thinking Activity is used before, during, and after reading. Before reading, students identify the purpose of reading and make a prediction about the content. Students write these predictions on the left-hand side of a two-column chart. During reading, students make additional predictions or verify or modify their original predictions. After reading, on the right-hand side of the two-column chart the students write evidence from the text that supports their prediction. Students then discuss the portions of the text that support their predictions.

K-W-L

This graphic organizer is particularly effective for activating students' background knowledge and setting a purpose for reading. On a large sheet of paper create a three-column chart. Label the first column K—for What I Know. Label the second column W—for What I Think I Will Learn or What I Want to Learn. Label the final column L—for What I Learned or Want to Learn More About. Before reading students complete the K and the W columns based upon what they already know about the topic and what they want to learn. After the reading they complete the L column indicating what they better understand now or new information they have learned. Following these steps reinforces what students have learned from the text while involving them in activities that good readers do.

Questioning the Author

This strategy involves discussion, instruction, and self-explanation by encouraging students to reflect on the author's meaning, motive, or purpose. Students respond to the teacher's questions such as the following: What is the author trying to say? What does the author mean? What is the author implying? To facilitate students' understanding, the teacher discusses what students can do when difficulties in comprehension occur. Students learn to "grapple" with text by emulating the teacher's questioning techniques.

Reciprocal Teaching

In reciprocal teaching teachers and students focus on a portion of the text through four guiding comprehension strategies: asking questions, clarifying difficult words and ideas, summarizing what has been read, and predicting what might come next. This activity is often completed in groups of four students where each student is responsible for one strategy. This process helps to identify difficulties students might have in using or applying specific strategies.

Transactional Strategy Instruction

In this process students construct meaning by setting goals and plans for reading, using background knowledge and text cues, monitor comprehension, solving problems, and evaluating their progress. These strategies include making predictions based on prior knowledge, generating and asking questions, clarifying, visualizing, relating background knowledge to the text, and summarizing. In a small group setting, these strategies form the basis of the dialog about the text as it is read aloud.

I-Chart

An I-Chart is a three-phase activity to encourage critical thinking about content-area texts. During the Planning Phase, students identify three content-area texts on a single topic. Students generate questions they want to find the answer to in their reading. Then they construct a chart to record information collected on the topic.

The next phase is the Interactive Phase where students record what they already know about the topic and any interesting facts they obtain from reading and rereading the sources. The final phase is the Integrating and Evaluating Phase. During this phase, students summarize, compare, research, and report on the topic.

Table 8.4   I-Chart (adapted from AdLit.org adlit.org/pdfs/strategy-library/ichart.pdf)

	I know . . .	*Question 1*	*Question 2*	*Question 3*	*Interesting Facts*	*New Questions*
Source 1						
Source 2						
Source 3						
Summary						

Topic: _____

REFERENCES

Biancarosa, G., & Snow, C. E. (2006). *Reading Next: A Vision for Action and Research in Middle and High School Literacy—A Report to Carnegie Corporation of New York* (2nd ed.). Washington, DC: Alliance for Excellent Education.

Bromley, K. (2007). Best practices in teaching writing. In L. B. Gambrell, L. M. Morrow, & M. Pressley (Eds.), *Best Practices in Literacy Instruction* (3rd ed.). New York City, NY: The Guilford Press.

Cisco, M. (2004). All students need to be writers. *The Reference Shelf*. Retrieved from http://www.pathstoliteracy.org/sites/pathstoliteracy.perkinsdev1.org/files/uploaded-files/db-LiteracyFocusWritingSkills.pdf.

Clay, M. M. (1998). *By Different Paths to Common Outcomes*. York, ME: Stenhouse.

Close, E., Hull, M., & Langer, J. (2006). Writing and reading relationships in literacy learning. In R. Indrisano & J. R. Paratore (Ed.), *Learning to Write Writing to Learn: Theory and Research in Practice* (pp. 176–192). Boston, MA: International Reading Association.

Englert, C. S. (1992). Writing instruction from a sociocultural perspective: The holistic, dialogic, and social enterprise of writing. *Journal of Learning Disabilities, 25*(3), 153–172. Retrieved from http://dx.doi.org/10.1177/002221949202500303.

Englert, C. S., Mariage, T. V., & Dunsmore, K. (2006). Tenets of sociocultural theory in writing instruction research. In C. A. MacArthur, S. Graham, & J. Fitzgerald (Eds.), *Handbook of Writing Research* (pp. 208–221). New York, NY: The Guilford Press.

Fisher, D., Frey, N., & ElWardi, R. (2006). Creating independent writers and thinkers in secondary schools. In R. Indrisano & J. R. Paratore (Ed.), *Learning to Write Writing to Learn: Theory and Research in Practice* (pp. 137–155). Boston, MA: International Reading Association.

Fitzgerald, J., & Shanahan, T. (2000). Reading and writing relations and their development. *Educational Psychologist, 35*(1), 39–50.

Frey, N. & Fisher, D. (2019). "You got more of these?" Reengaging adolescent readers and writers with meaningful texts. *Random House, Inc., 1*(1), 7–12. Retrieved from http://randomhouse.com/highschool/RHI_magazine/reluctant_readers/freyfisher.html.

Gallagher, K. (2019). *Building Deeper Readers & Writers*. Retrieved from http://www.kellygallagher.org/article-of-the-week.

Gibson, S. A. (2008, December). An effective framework for primary-grade guided writing instruction. *The Reading Teacher, 62*(4), 324–334.

Goldenberg, C. (1992). Instructional conversations: Promoting comprehension through discussion. *The Reading Teacher, 46*(4), 316–326. Retrieved from https://www.jstor.org/stable/20201075?seq=1/subjects.

Graham, S. (2006). Strategy instruction and the teaching of writing: A meta-analysis. In C. A. MacArthur, S. Graham, & J. Fitzgerald (Eds.), *Handbook of Writing Research* (pp. 187–207). New York City, NY: Guilford Press.

Graham, S., & Hebert, M. (2010). *Writing to Read: Evidence for How Writing can Improve Reading.* New York City, NY: Carnegie Corporation.

Graham, S., & Perin, D. (2007). *Writing Next: Effective Strategies to Improve Writing of Adolescents in Middle and High Schools.* New York City, NY: Carnegie Corporation.

Harris, K. R., & Graham, S. (1996). *Making the Writing Process Work: Strategies for Composition and Self-Regulation.* Brookline, MA: Brookline Books.

Hillocks, G. (1986). Research on written composition: New directions for teaching. Urbana, IL: National Conference on Research in English; ERIC Clearinghouse on Reading and Communication Skills. Retrieved from https://eric.ed.gov/?id=ED265552.

Loewus, L. H. (2016, February 25). After reading should students discuss the text or write about it? [Blog post]. Retrieved from https://blogs.edweek.org/edweek/curriculum/2016/02/after_reading_should_students_discuss_or_write.html.

Marzano, R. (2012, February). Writing to learn. *Educational Leadership, 69*(5), 82–83.

McKinney, C., Glazebrook, B., Sanders, J., & Shapiro, J. D. (2018). *AVID Writing for Disciplinary Literacy: A Schoolwide Approach.* San Diego, CA: AVID Press.

NCTE. (2016, February 28). Professional knowledge for the teaching of writing. Retrieved from http://www2.ncte.org/statement/teaching-writing/.

Richards & Strum. (n.d.). Writing instruction in primary classrooms: Implications for students with disabilities. Retrieved from file:///E:/Rowman%20and%20Littlefield/2121-Richards-Stephanie%20Primary%20Writing%20Instruction.pdf.

Russell, D. R. (2006). Historical studies on composition. In P. Smagorinsky (Ed.), *Research on Composition: Multiple Perspectives on Two Decades of Change* (pp. 243–275). New York City, NY: Teachers College Press.

Salahu-Din, D., Persky, H., & Miller, J. (2008). *The Nation's Report Card: Writing 2007.* NCES 2008–468. National Center for Education Statistics, Institute of Education Sciences, U.S. Department of Education, Washington, D.C.

Stowe, M. M. (2011, February/March). Reading + writing = stronger literacy skills. William & Mary School of Education Training & Technical Assistance. Retrieved from https://education.wm.edu/centers/ttac/resources/articles/teachtechnique/readingwritingliteracy/index.php.

Tompkins, G. E. (2017). *Literacy for the 21st Century: A Balanced Approach* (7th ed.). Boston, MA: Pearson Education, Inc.

Chapter 9

The Literacy Mosaic

After reading the chapters in this book, you will likely come to the conclusion that reading is a complex process. Good readers seamlessly use their knowledge of phonological awareness, phonics, and vocabulary to fluently read and comprehend text, but this is not an easy process for all students. Scarborough (2001) created an iconic visual of the reading process that illustrates that "reading is a multifaceted skill, gradually acquired over years of instruction and practice." This visual is often referred to as Scarborough's Reading Rope. The strands of the rope are divided into two basic categories: language comprehension and word recognition. Language comprehension, which becomes "increasingly strategic," includes background knowledge, vocabulary knowledge, language structures, verbal reasoning, and literacy knowledge. Word recognition, which becomes "increasingly automatic," includes phonological awareness, decoding (and spelling), and sight recognition. When the strands of the rope come together, skilled reading, fluent execution and coordination of word recognition, and text comprehension occur (Scarborough, 2001).

It has been our experience that struggling readers can be divided into two categories: those who struggle with the more foundational skills of decoding and fluency, and those who read fluently but experience difficulty with the comprehension process. Scarborough's illustration supports this thinking.

Students at all levels may struggle in one or multiple areas. Phonics and fluency problems are not limited to elementary students. Both middle and high school students can have deficits in these areas as well. Although it is not common for older students to have phonological issues, they do occur. Having students repeat, practice, and break words into syllables when being introduced to content vocabulary is a simple strategy that can be used to promote phonological awareness in older students. Phonics instruction for older students should not look the same as phonics instruction at the elementary level. Teaching older students how to decode multisyllabic words rather than simple, single-syllable words that are generally associated with elementary phonics instruction addresses fundamental phonics skills and, when taught correctly, can have a significant impact on the reading progress of older learners. Providing students with fix-up strategies for what to do when a word does not make sense and showing students how to use word parts such as prefixes, suffixes, bases, and roots that they recognize also help students decode unknown words. There is no easy solution for remedying the problems of our readers who struggle at the word level, but knowledgeable teachers, who are able to diagnose issues that struggling readers face, are also able to prescribe, construct, and present instruction to help those students succeed. Knowledgeable teachers at the secondary level do not assume that all reading issues are comprehension issues. Although comprehension issues are present, they know that it is sometimes necessary to dig deeper to find difficulties that may underlie the more obvious struggle with comprehension.

Struggling readers at the elementary, middle, and high school levels do not sound greatly different. The levels of text they are expected to read certainly vary, but decoding and fluency issues sound very similar in students of all ages.

Eleventh-grade student Carly was a B student. She was involved in many extracurricular activities and should have been college- or career-ready after high school, but there was one problem: she was unable to pass the state reading assessment necessary for graduation. A score concordant to a passing score on the state assessment, on either the ACT or the SAT, would have met the graduation requirement as well, but after multiple attempts she was not successful in passing any of these assessments at the necessary level.

One morning in her reading class I sat with her small group. Carly was reading aloud and after listening to her read for just five minutes, it became clear that she was unable to decode several of the words in her grade-level text. She read with expression, although not smoothly; she was able to answer knowledge-level questions about the text. She was even able to draw some basic conclusions. As I talked with her teacher, it became apparent that her teacher had not recognized Carly was having difficulty with both decoding and fluency. In her eleventh-grade reading class, they were working strictly on comprehension strategies.

For about six weeks, I worked with Carly individually on strategies for what to do when she came to a word she did not know. During this time, we worked on her fluency as well. After six weeks Carly did not become a completely proficient reader, but her reading showed vast improvement, and she passed the state assessment during the final assessment period just prior to graduation! During our instruction, she kept saying, "Why has no one ever taught me this before?" I can't say for sure that she was not taught the skills she needed to decode words because it was likely that someone had taught her these skills. My guess is that she was not developmentally ready at the time, and she was able to hide her reading deficit because she was able to compensate for her weak areas with her many strengths.

Recognizing the struggling reader who sounds fluent but is not comprehending proficiently is a challenge for all teachers. For these students, we need to be detectives; it is not easy to determine what is preventing our fluent readers from comprehending text. We don't hear the issue; we can't see the issue. For these students, we need to explore what it is they are not doing in their heads. The only way to do this is through conversation. Modeling what good readers do in their head as they read may be the best strategy for these students.

Recently, I visited a classroom where the teacher had students doing think alouds as they read text. I found it similar to a math teacher asking students to show their work. If we can understand what students are or are not doing to process the passage, we can guide them to use successful strategies that engage them with the text.

There is no magic wand to make the struggling reader suddenly proficie! Early intervention, lots and lots of reading, and plenty of opportunities to practice the skills you teach can have a significant impact on students' progress. However, we need to recognize that readers come to us with multiple literacies—visual, digital, technological, and beyond. We have students with cultural backgrounds and influences that we need to understand. We have students that lack motivation to learn to read for multiple reasons, and we need to find what motivates them. We need to understand that learning is a social process and provide opportunities for students to learn from one another.

In 1999, the American Federation of Teachers published a paper entitled "Teaching Reading *IS* Rocket Science," which truly sums it up. Teaching reading is a complex process that requires teachers who are knowledgeable about the reading process.

One of the shifts required of teachers with the advent of more rigorous standards involves increasing text complexity in the classroom. For students who are struggling readers, this means scaffolding the text so they can be successful. One way of achieving this is with repeated readings of a text for multiple purposes. When you consider that students are assessed with grade-level text, we are doing them a disservice by not teaching them how to read a text that may be a challenge for them. This is not to say that we should not give struggling readers texts that they can read independently. We need to do that as well. Ultimately, we need to put the right text in students' hands for the right purpose.

We also need to increase the amount of informational texts that we use for instruction. We need to challenge ourselves to find informational texts to complement literary texts that we are using in the classroom. This is one way of helping students make connections between the text they are reading, the world, and other texts.

I had the pleasure of hearing Lucy Calkins (2013) speak. Several things she said were notable, but I recall at one point her saying that in recent years there was not much text in conversations about text. I sat in the audience nodding my head vigorously. I recall vividly the trend to have students make personal connections to text, and much of the writing about text involved how it made the students feel. Text-based answers and writing to sources are additional shifts with the Common Core. Our students as writers and speakers need to be taught how to use evidence to inform or make an argument. When I think back to my college days, this was an expectation of every class, but I was ill-prepared for that type of reading and writing. If we begin preparing our students to use evidence from text in their speaking and writing from an early age, the transition to college expectations by the time they are in high school will go smoothly.

We need to make literacy a priority in all content areas. I have known teachers who put their entire curriculum on PowerPoint. Students view the PowerPoint, but they are never expected to read from a text to learn about the topic. We need to put text back into instruction and in the hands of students in all content areas. We need to incorporate literacy strategies to support our students as independent learners of our content. Along with this, academic vocabulary that supports our students across curriculums needs to be explicitly taught.

Finally, learning is a social process. The use of oral language through debates, conversations, Socratic seminars, or any speaking venue will help students bridge what they have learned from their reading and organize and internalize their new understandings.

One of the greatest achievements of the more rigorous standards is that they have made us reflect on our instructional practices. Teaching is a reflective practice that requires us to constantly rethink and revamp to find a better way to help students achieve literacy and learning success. You make the difference for your students! Help them be successful readers, writers, and thinkers.

REFERENCES

Calkins, L. (2013). *Pathways to the Common Core: Accelerating Achievement.* Retrieved from readingandwritingproject.com/public/.../TC_pathways_seminar.pdf.

Scarborough, H. (2001). The many strands that are woven into skilled reading. Retrieved from http://www.ncsip.org/reading/Rope-Model-of-Skilled-Reading-Scarborough.pptx.

Index

About the Authors

Lin Carver is the director of Program Approval and the Reading Program Administrator at Saint Leo University. She presents nationally and internationally and instructs and designs courses in literacy, technology, and instructional leadership.

Lauren Pantoja is a Learning Design Coach at Paul R. Smith Middle School in Pasco County, Florida, and was recognized as the Florida Literacy Coach of the Year. She works as an adjunct instructor at Saint Leo University preparing future literacy teachers and coaches.

Lin and Lauren have been working together for over a decade making a difference by advocating for literacy mastery for learners of all ages.